...mber 25, 1942.

Dear Jacqueline,

I am writing this letter in order to bid you good-bye. That will probably surprise you, but fate has decreed that I must leave (as you will of course have heard a long time ago) with my family, for reasons you will know.

When you telephoned me on Sunday afternoon I couldn't say anything, for my mother had told me not to, the whole house was upside down, and the front door was locked. Hello was due to come, but we didn't answer the door. I can't write to everyone and that's why I'm just writing to you. I'm taking it that you won't talk to anybody about the letter nor from whom you got it. I would be so grateful if you would be really nice and keep up a secret correspondence with me. I hope we'll meet again soon, but it probably won't be before the end of the war. Later, of course, you'll be able to tell people that you had a farewell letter from me. Well then, Jackie, I hope things go well with you, that I hear from you soon and that we'll meet again soon.

Your <u>best</u> friend,

<u>Anne</u>

One girl's story of war, peace, and

a unique friendship with Anne Frank

A Friend Called
ANNE

JACQUELINE VAN MAARSEN

retold for children by Carol Ann Lee

PUFFIN BOOKS

PUFFIN

Published by the Penguin Group

Penguin Young Readers Group,

345 Hudson Street, New York, New York 10014, U.S.A.

Penguin Group (Canada), 90 Eglinton Avenue East, Suite 700, Toronto, Ontario, Canada M4P 2Y3
(a division of Pearson Penguin Canada Inc.)

Penguin Books Ltd, 80 Strand, London WC2R 0RL, England

Penguin Ireland, 25 St Stephen's Green, Dublin 2, Ireland (a division of Penguin Books Ltd)

Penguin Group (Australia), 250 Camberwell Road, Camberwell, Victoria 3124, Australia
(a division of Pearson Australia Group Pty Ltd)

Penguin Books India Pvt Ltd, 11 Community Centre, Panchsheel Park, New Delhi - 110 017, India

Penguin Group (NZ), Cnr Airborne and Rosedale Roads, Albany, Auckland 1310, New Zealand
(a division of Pearson New Zealand Ltd)

Penguin Books (South Africa) (Pty) Ltd, 24 Sturdee Avenue, Rosebank, Johannesburg 2196, South Africa

Registered Offices: Penguin Books Ltd, 80 Strand, London WC2R 0RL, England

First published in the U.K. by Penguin Books Ltd, 2004
First published in the United States of America by Viking,
a division of Penguin Young Readers Group, 2005
Published by Puffin, a division of Penguin Young Readers Group, 2007

1 3 5 7 9 10 8 6 4 2

THE LIBRARY OF CONGRESS HAS CATALOGED THE VIKING EDITION AS FOLLOWS:
Lee, Carol Ann. A friend called Anne / by Jacqueline van Maarsen;
retold for children by Carol Ann Lee.
p. cm.
ISBN: 0-670-05958-7 (hc)
1. Frank, Anne, 1929–1945. 2. Maarsen, Jacqueline van.
3. Jews—Netherlands—Amsterdam—Biography—Juvenile literature.
4. Holocaust, Jewish (1939–1945)—Netherlands—Amsterdam—Biography—Juvenile literature.
5. Amsterdam (Netherlands)—Biography—Juvenile literature.
I. Maarsen, Jacqueline van. Anne en Jopie. II. Title.
DS135.N6F73392 2005
940.53'18'092—dc22
[B]
2004021418

Puffin Books ISBN 978-0-14-240719-6

Printed in the United States of America

Photographs copyright © Jacqueline van Maarsen, 2005
Photographs of Anne Frank copyright © Getty Images, Hulton Archive

To my sister, Christiane
—J.V.M.

OTHER BOOKS YOU MAY ENJOY

Anne Frank: A Hidden Life	Mirjam Pressler
Anne Frank: Beyond the Diary	Tony Langham, Ruud Van der Rol, Rian Verhoeven
Behind the Secret Window	Nelly S. Toll
The Devil's Arithmetic	Jane Yolen
The Final Journey	Gudrun Pausewang, Patricia Crampton
Hide and Seek	Ida Vos, Terese Edelstein, Inez Smidt
I Am a Star: Child of the Holocaust	Inge Auerbacher
Malka	Mirjam Pressler
The Night Journey	Kathryn Lasky
Stones in Water	Donna Jo Napoli

CONTENTS

PREFACE ix

INTRODUCTION 1

PROLOGUE: Best Friends 7

CHAPTER 1: The Road to War 15

CHAPTER 2: Anne 33

CHAPTER 3: Getting to Know Each Other 51

CHAPTER 4: Separation 61

CHAPTER 5: Removing the Yellow Star 79

CHAPTER 6: Last Good-byes 95

CHAPTER 7: The Hunger Winter 107

CHAPTER 8: Liberation 121

CHAPTER 9: The Diary of Anne Frank 137

CHAPTER 10: Fame 153

TIMELINE OF IMPORTANT EVENTS IN THE

NETHERLANDS 159

PREFACE

One day, while I was talking to children about my experiences during the Second World War and about my friendship with Anne Frank, a small boy asked me, "Why didn't you just fly away in an airplane?" I suddenly realized how difficult it must be for young children living at the beginning of the twenty-first century to imagine what it was like living in Holland in the 1940s during the German occupation. A situation without freedom, without any communication with the outside world, and, in the last years of the war, without means of transportation—no trains, no boats, no cars, not even bicycles. Airplanes we could see only high in the sky: the Allied forces on their way to attack German targets.

We were prisoners in our own country, and it was very difficult for those people opposing the Nazis by joining the Resistance not to get caught. And at the same time it was very easy for the Nazis to round up the Jewish people and send them to the concentration camps with the intention of killing them all.

Anne Frank's diary leaves a very strong message, a message directed against discrimination. It shows the results when discrimination against ethnic groups is pushed to its extremes. The only way to avoid such catastrophes from happening again is to inform young people today about what happened during the war. One cannot work on the future without knowledge of the past. Anne Frank became a legend. And having been Anne's best friend, I became part of that legend. That's why I wrote a book about this friendship and give talks about her fate and the fate of others. I am glad that Carol Ann Lee has retold my story for children since it not only paints a picture of what it was like for me to grow up during the Second World War, but also gives young people an insight into the terrible years of the Nazi occupation and the Holocaust.

Jacqueline van Maarsen

A Friend Called
ANNE

Jacqueline (right) and her sister, Christiane, with
their maid, Rika, at the entrance of their home.

INTRODUCTION

I was eight years old when I first read Anne Frank's *Diary* and ten when I saw Otto Frank, Anne's father, being interviewed on BBC TV's *Blue Peter*. Seeing and hearing Mr. Frank made an enormous impression upon me because, although I knew that the diary was real, it was amazing to think that someone connected to it was still alive somewhere in this world. To me, the events that Anne Frank wrote about in her diary seemed very, very long ago—far more distant than they really were. The peculiar thing was that Anne herself didn't seem like a historical figure at all; the diary kept her alive and continues to do so for millions of readers. Apart from her exceptional gift for writing, she could have been any girl I knew, and the friendships she had before going into hiding were just like my own, which made it even more impossible to understand why she and millions of other Jews were murdered.

It was this need to understand that led me to read everything I could find on Anne Frank, and the times in which she lived. Although I found a great deal, I still felt there was far more to learn. The books, articles, and films told me a lot, but not enough. When I was eighteen I decided I would write a biography about Anne Frank myself, but it wasn't until ten years later that I actually began to write it in the way I imagined it should be written. It was accepted for publication, and I then set out on Anne's trail, locating where she had lived, the schools she had attended, her hiding place, the places she had been imprisoned in and, most importantly, the people she had known.

I don't remember every detail of my first meeting with Jacqueline van Maarsen, Anne's best friend and the girl whom she called "Jopie" in the diary. But what I haven't forgotten is how strange it seemed, to be sitting in Jacqueline's lovely home in Amsterdam with its view across the city, and her husband, Ruud, bringing us cups of tea as she and I chatted. Although I was twenty-eight then, I could still hear the voice of my eight-year-old self in my head exclaiming, "I'm talking to Anne Frank's best friend!" It was an odd moment, too, when Jacqueline showed me her copy of the first-ever edition of Anne's diary, with its personal note from Otto Frank. I had already seen photographs of Jacqueline around the time of her friendship with Anne, and I was surprised how little she had changed over the years. It made me wonder how Anne would have looked, if she had lived, and if she would have had children and grandchildren, as Jacqueline did.

Although I was then most curious about Jacqueline's many memories of Anne, I quickly understood that Jacqueline herself had a very interesting story to tell. She had written a book about her friendship with Anne, which was published in the Netherlands and America, but I wondered why she didn't write more about her own life, which was fascinating quite apart from the relationship with Anne Frank. The problem was that Jacqueline didn't realize how interesting her past was, and this, together with her reluctance to talk about herself, meant that no one really knew much about her. But we began working on this book, and I am so glad that we did, because I think Jacqueline's story is a very unusual one and hopefully it will capture you as much as it did me.

When you've finished this book, you might wonder about Jacqueline's life now. She still lives in Amsterdam, with her husband, but in a different apartment from the one where I first met her. And she is a happy mother and proud grandmother too. Is she much like the "Jopie" we all know from the diary? Well, yes, I think she is. Although Jacqueline is shy, she's a very good talker and an excellent listener. She once told me that one of the things she liked most about Anne was her honesty, and that's a quality Jacqueline shares too. She's very direct, which is probably useful when answering the questions people put to her about Anne. Since writing her first book, Jacqueline has written another, which was published in the Netherlands recently (where it was a success), and she gives several talks a year to groups who want to know about Anne, about her, and about the war in general. Her husband attends these talks with her, and usually speaks too, since he was in hiding, like Anne, during the war. However, he was not in hiding with his parents, but all alone in a family who did not know him.

Jacqueline is still a collector, although now she collects different editions of Anne's diary, and has a bookcase full of them. On more than one occasion, after chatting away with Jacqueline for a while, I've been suddenly struck again by the fact that I am talking to "Jopie." Then I always ask, "Doesn't it feel strange to think that the girl who was your best friend is now so famous?" Jacqueline's answer is always, "Yes, of course. Because to me she was just Anne, my school friend.

And to see her become this icon . . . yes, it is strange."

In the letter she wrote to Jacqueline from her hiding place, Anne noted, "Later, of course, you'll be able to tell people that you had a farewell letter from me." In this book, Jacqueline tells us not only about the letter and her friendship with Anne Frank, but—and just as importantly—about her own, extraordinary life.

Carol Ann Lee

High above the canals of Amsterdam, in a cramped, dusty attic filled with boxes and washing hung up to dry on the old wooden beams, a young girl was writing a letter to her best friend. Outside, the late summer sun shone on the oily water of the Prinsengracht Canal, and seagulls glided over the orange rooftops of the city as the bells of the nearby church, the Westerkerk, chimed the hour.

> *Dear Jacqueline,*
> *I am writing this letter in order to bid you good-bye. That will probably surprise you, but fate has decreed that I must leave (as you will of course have heard a long time ago) with my family, for reasons you will know.*
> *When you telephoned me on Sunday afternoon I couldn't say anything, for my mother had told me not*

to, the whole house was upside down and the front
door was locked. . . . I can't write to everyone and
that's why I'm just writing to you. I'm taking it that
you won't talk to anybody about the letter nor from
whom you got it. I would be so grateful if you would
be really nice and keep up a secret correspondence with
me. All enquiries to Mrs. Gies!!!! I hope we'll meet
again soon, but it probably won't be before the end of
the war. If Lies or anyone else asks you if you've heard
anything from me say absolutely nothing, otherwise
you'll get us and Mrs. Gies into mortal trouble, so I
hope you'll be really careful. Later, of course, you'll be
able to tell people that you had a farewell letter from
me. . . .

It was September 25, 1942. Thirteen-year-old Anne Frank had been in hiding with her parents, her older sister, Margot, and another family for three months. Two years before, the Nazis had invaded the Netherlands, and they began persecuting Jews there just as they had in Germany and all the other European countries that were under Nazi rule. In summer 1942, the deportation of Jews to concentration camps got under way. Although those who were sent to the camps did not know what to expect, everyone was aware that something terrible was happening in those distant, secretive places. When sixteen-year-old Margot received the call-up to report for work in one of these camps, her parents took action immediately. For the past twelve months, they had been preparing a hiding place in the old annex behind Mr. Frank's business premises, and now the time had come to "dive under," as the Dutch called it: to disappear from normal life, leaving no trace of where they had gone. They moved swiftly, and Anne was forced to leave behind almost everything she owned: her little cat Moortje, books, games, some of her favorite clothes, and many other possessions that made life enjoyable.

Worst of all for a lively, sociable girl like Anne, she was no longer able to have any contact with her friends, because that would have been too dangerous. Apart from the four people who worked in Mr. Frank's offices and took care of them, no one was allowed to know where they were hiding. Anne found the situation very difficult to handle at first and was very lonely, for she had always had a large circle of friends. At the center of that circle was her best friend, Jacqueline van Maarsen. Since their first meeting in September 1941 at the Jewish Lyceum in Amsterdam, they had been inseparable. Despite the fact that Jacqueline was a more reserved girl than Anne, they both had the same interests and spent hours chatting, playing games, reading their favorite books together, and looking through their collections of movie-star postcards. They stayed overnight at each other's houses, visited the local ice-cream shop to see who else was hanging around there, and were in the same class at school.

As the weather got warmer, they often climbed out of a window onto the flat roof behind Anne's house (a small gravel area they called "the terrace") and sat together in the sun, telling each other secrets they would never dream of telling anyone else. Anne talked a lot about boys, especially the ones she thought wanted to go for a walk with her and chat. Sometimes she talked about her family; she thought her father was perfect, but didn't get along very well with her mother and was annoyed that everyone thought her sister, Margot, was more talented and beautiful than she was. Anne was quite vain, since she knew that she was attractive, and was always brushing her thick, shiny black hair, which she believed to be her best feature. Jacqueline was pretty too, with huge blue eyes that Anne envied. Sometimes the two of them discussed their plans for after the war—the parties they would go to; the places they would see; the people they would meet.

Although the anti-Jewish laws meant that there were few activities open to them, Jacqueline and Anne still had a lot of fun together, and in the early summer of 1942, they formed a table-tennis club with some other girls. They played the game at their friend Ilse's house, on the table in the dining room, and gave their club a name: the Little Bear Minus 2. The five members of the club named themselves after the constellation the Little Bear, which they thought was made up of five stars, only to find out afterward that it actually has seven—hence the "Minus 2." They laughed a lot about the silly name.

When Anne and Jacqueline weren't playing table tennis, they sometimes arranged cinema afternoons at Anne's house on the weekend. Mr. Frank was in charge of the projector that showed the films, and Mrs. Frank was given the job of handing out refreshments. Anne and Jacqueline were the usherettes, and only people who had been invited were allowed in; they had to hand in the tickets that Anne and Jacqueline had made so that it had the atmosphere of a proper movie theater. For Anne's thirteenth birthday, a month before she went into hiding, there had been a party and a film. It was one of the best days Anne and Jacqueline ever had together. Anne was very proud of the diary she had received from her parents as her main gift, and showed it to everyone. After she began writing in it, though, she wouldn't let anyone see it, not even Jacqueline, her best friend. The diary was one of the few things she was allowed to take to the secret annex.

It was around this time that Anne and Jacqueline made a pact. They would always be best friends, no matter what happened, but everything was so uncertain now that the Nazis were stepping up their persecution of Jews. Jews began to disappear, sometimes voluntarily to escape the Nazis, but more often they were seized without warning. This had already happened to Jacqueline's cousin David; no one heard from him again until a card arrived for his mother. It said David had died in Mauthausen, a concentration camp in Austria, far away from Amsterdam. With these sorts of events in mind, Anne and Jacqueline promised each other that if one of them had to go away suddenly, then each would write the other a letter of farewell. Anne wrote to Jacqueline from the secret annex, but it wasn't until after the war that Jacqueline was able to read the letter.

On that September afternoon in 1942, Anne was ending her letter just as someone called her name from below. The office workers had gone home, and now everyone in the prisonlike annex could move about a little more freely at least. However, none of them could go farther than the door to the main building, which had been concealed by a bookcase on the other side.

The shadows in the attic were starting to lengthen, and soon it would be night, when every sound from outside seemed doubly threatening and could mean that their hiding place had been discovered. Anne closed her mind to such thoughts and wrote the last few lines of her letter to Jacqueline, knowing that she could never send it and that it would remain tucked inside the pages of her diary:

> *Well then, Jackie, I hope things go well with you, that I hear from you soon and that we'll meet again soon.*
> *Your _best_ friend,*
> *_Anne_*
> *P.S. I hope that we'll always stay _best_ friends until we meet again.*

Anne folded the letter and placed it inside her diary. The sunlight had gone from the room. Through the tiny attic window she could see that the sky behind the tall tower of the Westerkerk, with its distinctive golden crown, had grown dark. She closed the diary and walked over to the short flight of stairs, where the hum of voices reached her from the floor below.

The van Maarsens' home at Willemsparkweg, Amsterdam.
The entrance is the third door from the right.

CHAPTER 1

THE ROAD TO WAR

Eleven-year-old Jacqueline van Maarsen awoke suddenly, unable to understand at first what had disturbed her dreams. Then she heard it again: a strange droning noise, like thousands of huge bees flying by. She rubbed her eyes, wondering if she was still dreaming. The clock on her bedside table told her that it was almost four in the morning. She knew that she was awake; the moonlight shone brightly through the curtains, illuminating every piece of furniture and all the toys and books in her bedroom. She realized that the noise was real, and that it was getting louder.

Suddenly there were a number of tremendous explosions that seemed to shake the city apart. Jacqueline was more shocked than frightened as she jumped up and padded over to the window. As she moved aside the curtains, her eyes widened in disbelief: massive

airplanes were streaming over the orange-slate rooftops of Amsterdam, their wings silver under the moon.
Somewhere in the distance, fires burned; Jacqueline
could smell the smoke and see the vivid glow on the
horizon. Then a single plane came tearing by, much
faster than the rest, emptying its guns over the violent
landscape that Jacqueline no longer recognized as the
city in which she lived. The smoky sky was filled with
an incredible fury. Jacqueline turned and ran to her
parents' room, meeting her older sister, Christiane, in
the hall.

"Papa, what's happening?"

Mr. van Maarsen looked pale and drawn. "They're
German planes, Jackie. It looks as though the Netherlands is being taken over by the Nazis, just as we feared.
Try not to panic; we'll know for certain soon enough,"
he said.

The airplanes kept coming until daybreak. As soon
as it was light, Jacqueline sat down with her parents and
Christiane to listen to the radio. The solemn voice of
the announcer crackled across the airwaves: "This is it.
Our country is being invaded."

It was Friday, May 10, 1940, and German forces
were attacking the Netherlands, Belgium, and France
simultaneously.

Although it was a school day, it was unthinkable

that anyone should attend when everything was in such an uproar. The streets thronged with worried-looking people talking in high, excitable tones about the invasion. Jacqueline went outside with her mother and listened to their conversations.

"The Nazis are landing by parachutes."

"My neighbor told me that boats are in the harbor waiting for Jews who want to go to England while they still can. They're the ones who have the most to fear, as we all know."

"The radio says to hide any alcohol because German soldiers go crazy when they've been drinking."

It seemed to Jacqueline as though everyone was talking at once, and she could barely understand much of what was said. No one knew the truth about anything, but everyone repeated the rumors that they had heard. Eventually, Jacqueline and her mother returned home, but every five minutes someone would knock on their door.

"Heard anything new, Mr. van Maarsen?"

"Did you make any plans for what to do in the event of a German invasion?"

"Perhaps it's not the Netherlands they want, Mrs. van Maarsen. Perhaps this is some sort of test."

Shortly before lunchtime, a penetrating wail filled the skies. It was an air-raid siren, warning everyone to take cover from falling bombs. Still stunned by what had already happened, Jacqueline rushed down to the cellar with her sister and parents. Fear made them all silent, unable to think of anything to say. It was cold, and the place smelled faintly of damp concrete. They sat there for a long while, until the all-clear signal sounded, and then they allowed themselves the relief of talking.

"Come on upstairs, everyone," said Jacqueline's mother, leading the way.

The danger of being bombed had passed, but only temporarily.

That afternoon, Jacqueline and Christiane watched their mother sticking strips of brown paper over the windows.

"What are they for?" Jacqueline asked.

"To help prevent the glass from shattering if bombs fall," Mrs. van Maarsen said, applying the last of the paper to the windows.

Jacqueline peeped out between the strips. Virtually every house in the street now looked the same, with strange brown crosses on every piece of glass.

"We should do something useful too," Jacqueline told her sister.

Christiane thought for a minute before saying, "I know, let's buy sweets and chocolate and put it all away safely. Maybe we won't be allowed to buy them any-more if the Germans take over."

They rushed out to buy as many sweets as they could afford between them. Although Jacqueline thought the idea was a bit mad, she felt she was doing something that might prove practical later. They placed the small pile of sweets in a shoebox and closed the cardboard lid firmly.

"Put it under your bed," Christiane instructed.

Jacqueline pushed the box into the narrow space beneath her bed, wondering how long their supplies would last.

The evening passed slowly. People who had gone to work as usual returned home exhausted with worry. Jacqueline watched a Jewish family she knew waiting for the tram to Central Station, and she wondered if they were going to try and board one of the boats in the harbor of Ijmuiden. She remembered what the woman in the street had said earlier about Jewish people: "They're the ones who have the most to fear." Jacqueline felt frightened; although her mother was Catholic, her father was Jewish—were the Nazis going to do something to him? And what about her Jewish uncles, aunts, and cousins—what was going to happen to them? Jacqueline had seen newsreels in the cinema about Nazi Germany and how Jews there were treated, and she had grown used to large numbers of German Jewish refugees arriving in the neighborhood. Some of the refugees attended her school, but since they never talked about their experiences before coming to the Netherlands, Jacqueline didn't like to ask. In any case, the Netherlands seemed to offer them protection. Or so everyone had thought. She climbed into bed that night overcome with fear and uncertainty, wondering what was going to happen next. She stared into the darkness for a long time. Perhaps they would flee too, on a boat, to another country where the Nazis couldn't reach them. She pulled the covers over her head, wishing the Nazis would just go away and leave them in peace.

For the next few days, Jacqueline felt as though she was living in the center of a whirlwind. She and her family continued to do things as they had always done them, but it was as if time had been suspended, for no one knew what lay ahead. The country itself was in chaos. On Sunday, May 12, a bomb fell on Amsterdam, killing fifty-one people. The airport and the docks were on fire; it was beautiful weather and the flames roared up to the sun. The radio reported that the Dutch royal family and government had escaped to England. Everyone felt betrayed and angry that the royals and the politicians had simply abandoned them to their fate.

"It's dreadful, appalling," Jacqueline heard her mother's friend say.

"But what use would they be here?" Mr. van Maarsen murmured. "The Germans would have arrested them anyway—they might even have killed them all."

The news about the Dutch royal family and government was forgotten when the Germans threatened to destroy the port of Rotterdam unless the Netherlands surrendered. Before the deadline was due to expire, the Germans bombed Rotterdam, virtually razing the city to the ground.

"Thousands are dead and many more have been made homeless by the attack." Jacqueline listened to the newsreader, whose professional voice sounded muffled with emotion.

"Does this mean that the Germans are in charge now?" Christiane looked from her father to her mother.

"Let's just wait and see," Mr. van Maarsen said, with a calmness he probably didn't feel.

On May 15, it was all over. The Netherlands surrendered and was officially placed under German rule. Jacqueline stood with her family in the crowds watching the German troops enter Amsterdam. Under clear blue skies, the Germans passed by, grinning and waving in the brilliant sunshine, the Nazi flag flying from every vehicle. Some of the crowd ran out to shake the

Germans' hands, or gave the Hitler salute. Others stood with faces like stone, or turned away to hide the tears of anger, fear, and frustration that pricked their eyelids at the appalling scene of the Netherlands under Nazi rule.

Until the German invasion, Jacqueline's life had been happy and carefree. Her first few years were spent in a lovely house on Willemsparkweg, a quiet street between Amsterdam's biggest park, the Vondelpark, and the Museumplein, the square where the art museums stood. The kitchen window was below street level, and Jacqueline thought it was funny to watch the legs of people passing by, especially when it was raining, for then the legs went very fast! At the back of the house was a large garden, and the trees of the park could be seen from the upper rooms. Jacqueline and Christiane played in the spacious sitting-room during the daytime, under the watchful eye of their nanny. Upstairs, in two very elegantly decorated rooms, their mother worked at her business, buying designs and fabrics at the fashion shows in Paris and making and selling dresses in Amsterdam to well-to-do clients. "Don't come up here," Mrs. van Maarsen would warn. "I'm expecting a client today and mustn't be disturbed."

Mr. van Maarsen had his own room upstairs too, where he worked for his import-export company. So although Jacqueline and Christiane didn't see their parents during the day, they always knew that they were never far away. Not that this would have troubled Jacqueline anyway, since even when young she was a very easygoing little girl who felt no need to cling to her mother or to have constant attention. Christiane, on the other hand, made a fuss about everything. When Jacqueline had to go into the hospital to have her appendix taken out, Christiane wept and fretted, and kept asking their mother, "Is Jackie going to be all right? When is she coming home?" Jacqueline herself didn't make any fuss. "It's got to be done," she told herself, "so there's no point in upsetting everyone."

Despite the differences in their characters, Jacqueline and Christiane looked alike. Both girls were very slim with large, expressive eyes (Jacqueline's were blue and Christiane's were brown), and they both had dark, glossy hair, which their mother liked to tie up with bows and barrettes. Most of their clothes were made in their mother's fashion house, and Jacqueline remembers, "We loved her very much, but sometimes she was a bit difficult for us, because she always wanted us to look neat and behave as perfectly as possible. She was a very strong person. People liked and admired her because she always seemed to have a solution to any problem and had a fearless way about her. My father was much quieter, and I think he might have been an artist if he had ever had the opportunity to be one."

It was Mr. van Maarsen who took the keenest interest in his children's upbringing and education. Mrs. van Maarsen was usually occupied with her work, and because she was French and had moved to the Netherlands only after marrying Jacqueline's father, she found it hard to adapt to the Dutch language and way of life. Mr. van Maarsen decided to send his daughters to a Montessori school, feeling that the Montessori practice of allowing children to work on their own or in a small group in a relaxed atmosphere would suit them best. Jacqueline liked the school her father had chosen and made many friends there. Some of the pupils were Jewish children who had fled Nazi Germany with their parents. Jacqueline remembers, "When we were very young, we were not told much about the threat of the Nazis in Germany. As children, we thought Germany was far away, and it never occurred to us that the Nazis would come to the Netherlands. But I was aware that there were now lots of German Jewish children in the neighborhood and at school. That became more obvious when we moved to Albrecht Dürerstraat, in a different area. Our new home was an even shorter walk from school than before—only five minutes—I liked that!"

The new neighborhood, near an elegant shopping street called Beethovenstraat, was just as pleasant as their old one. All the houses were made of brown brick with white window frames and orange-tiled roofs, and people took pride in keeping their homes clean and attractive. The wide windows that looked out onto the street were always filled with plants and ornaments, and everyone was friendly to each other. Jacqueline recalls another reason why she liked it there: "Nearby were sites marked out for new houses to be built and the empty plots were like giant sandpits! We loved to play there and we called it the 'Sahara,' because it reminded us of the desert." Today Jacqueline lives in an apartment on that very spot, but it was not built until after 1945 because the war prevented the new houses from being constructed.

It was while playing in the "Sahara" that Jacqueline met a girl called Bertie, who lived nearby. Bertie saw Jacqueline throwing a ball into the air and called out, "Can you juggle as well?" From then on they became good friends, and when Jacqueline went along to the Brownies (a group for young girls), she invited Bertie to go with her. Afterward they both went to Bertie's grandmother's house and Bertie said that she wanted to join the Brownies too, like Jacqueline. Bertie's older sister laughed. "The Brownies—huh! That's stupid. *I* am going to become a member of the Jeugdstorm."

Jacqueline and Bertie stared at her in shock: the Jeugdstorm was a Nazi organization for young people. Bertie's grandmother was furious at her remark and shouted, "I absolutely forbid you to join *them*!" A huge argument followed, but later Jacqueline discovered Bertie's sister had gotten her own way after all: "I saw her walking along the street wearing the orange-and-black Jeugdstorm cap. After a while, I didn't see Bertie again, but I did catch sight of her father one day after the war had broken out. He was dressed in the sinister black uniform of the NSB, the Dutch Nazi Party."

Jacqueline's parents were always very busy, but they liked to take their daughters on holidays to the Belgian coast and tried to spend most summer weekends at Zandvoort, a seaside resort popular with the residents of Amsterdam. The beach was soft and white, and the sea was safe for paddling and swimming. Once a year they traveled to Paris to visit Mrs. van Maarsen's family. They saw a great deal of Mrs. van Maarsen's brother, who had no children and was very fond of Jacqueline and Christiane. When they went to Paris in 1937, he treated them to a boat trip down the river Seine. Immaculately dressed in white sailor dresses and white gloves, which were very fashionable then, Jacqueline and Christiane found the whole experience thrilling. They also loved visiting the Eiffel Tower, from where they could gaze at the wide spread of Paris far below.

Much of Jacqueline's time was taken up with birthday parties of friends and of her father's family; in the Netherlands everyone made a great fuss of celebrating birthdays. Lots of people would arrive at the home of the birthday boy or girl, and the entire day was spent playing games, eating little cakes, drinking, and opening presents. Every Sunday morning, Mr. van Maarsen would take his daughters to the cinema. It was near Rembrandtplein, a large square surrounded by cafés and bars. Jacqueline loved to watch *Popeye* and the other cartoons, but she tried to ignore the newsreels that accompanied every film, because the frenzied speeches of Adolf Hitler made her feel very nervous. To see the dark-haired, mustached, and scowling German leader shaking his fist in front of thousands of adoring followers and shouting that Jews were "evil" and had to be "stopped in their plans to take over the world" was very frightening. Jacqueline couldn't understand every word of Hitler's ranting, but she could sense the anger and hatred he preached. She glanced at her father for comfort, but Mr. van Maarsen always watched the news avidly and never took his eyes off the screen. Sometimes, when they came out of the cinema, Jacqueline asked her father, "What will Hitler *do*, Papa?"

Mr. van Maarsen's reply was always reassuring: "Don't worry, Jackie. We're safe here. Even if Hitler goes to war—which some people are saying he might— it's highly unlikely that he'll invade the Netherlands. This country has managed to avoid war for a very long time, so just try to forget about it."

Sometimes Jacqueline heard bits of conversations between her parents and their friends. Her mother always said the same thing: "It's so terrible. Why are they doing this? What is going to happen next?" Jacqueline would then listen to her father calming his wife down: "We just have to wait and hope for the best. Don't worry. Take things day by day. What else can we do?" Afterward Jacqueline would feel nervous, although she didn't understand exactly what was going on, only that the situation in Germany was unbearable. She remembers, "I got to know some of the German children who came to live in our neighborhood, but I didn't hear any stories about the situation they had left behind. I think they just wanted to adapt quickly to the Dutch customs and language." Jacqueline's parents tried to protect their daughters by keeping quiet about Germany as much as possible.

Within the next few months, however, the situation worsened. In November 1938, there was a mass attack on Jews all over Germany. Hundreds were killed; thousands were sent to concentration camps; and their homes, their businesses, and the synagogues where they worshipped were destroyed. Kristallnacht (the "Night of Broken Glass," so called because the streets were filled with shattered glass from targeted shops and houses) made front-page news all around the world. Now everyone could see that Jewish people who lived under the Nazi government were in grave danger. Thousands of Jews fled Germany after Kristallnacht, and many settled in the Netherlands.

In September 1939, after Germany invaded Poland, Britain and France declared war on Hitler. The Germans already occupied Austria and parts of the former Czechoslovakia, and in April 1940 they invaded Denmark and Norway. Even children as young as Jacqueline were aware that the Nazi menace was edging closer and closer. "Are we next?" Jacqueline sometimes asked herself anxiously. "Will the Nazis come for us too?" She said nothing about her fears to anyone, but she decided she had to do something to try to prevent an invasion from taking place. One day she got an idea:

she would make a doll with magic powers that would save the Netherlands from a German attack. She asked her mother to buy her some modeling clay to play with and then used it to make a figure with a large, round head and sticking-out legs and arms. It wasn't very artistic, but that didn't matter. What counted was its powers, and she concentrated on the doll for a long time, until she was certain that it really did hold magic within its weird little body.

Now we are safe, Jacqueline thought, staring at the doll determinedly. No one can harm us as long as I have this doll.

She stored it away carefully, taking it out only very rarely, to see if its magical powers were still intact. When she was sure they were, she put the doll back in its secret place.

But in May 1940 the Germans invaded and the Netherlands surrendered. A few days later, Jacqueline's mother arrived home very upset. When Mr. van Maarsen asked her what was the matter, she said in a low voice, "Our local baker has killed himself. And not on his own—the rest of his family are dead as well. They found that a better alternative to waiting to see what the Nazis have planned for the Jews here."

Jacqueline leaned against the wall, aghast. She knew the baker; he was a very friendly Jewish man who had fled Germany years before. She saw him every day with his cart of bread and pastries; he had always had a kind word and a smile for her. It just didn't seem possible that he was dead.

Jacqueline left the room and went upstairs to where the clay doll was hidden in her bedroom. She pulled it out and looked at it in disgust. So much for its magical powers. It was just a stupid, ugly doll. She went outside with it, walking to the nearest canal, where she threw the useless thing into the water. It floated, briefly, its arms and legs bobbing about on the dark surface for several minutes before it began to sink headfirst into the murky depths.

Jacqueline at school, around the time
she and Anne became friends.

CHAPTER 2

ANNE

The Germans began to bring in anti-Jewish laws very soon after seizing power in the Netherlands. The first laws affected adults more than children—at least that was how it felt to Jacqueline. Slowly, though, she saw how her life was changing in ways that she didn't like but was powerless to prevent. Rika, the van Maarsens' non-Jewish maid, was forced to leave the family after ten years with them. Mrs. van Maarsen's fashion house, which sold the clothes made by Mrs. van Maarsen, closed down because most people didn't have money to spend on expensive outfits. Moreover, the non-Jewish girls who used to work for her were forced to leave, just like Rika. Jacqueline could see how troubled her parents were, not only by the differences in their lifestyle, but also by the uncertainty of what the future would bring.

Mr. van Maarsen turned his hobby of collecting old books and prints into a business, but it did not pay well. One day Jacqueline's mother told her daughters just how serious the situation had become: "We can't go on living in this house. We can't afford it anymore. So we're going to sell some of the furniture and find a smaller place."

"But we'll still live in Amsterdam, won't we?" Jacqueline asked in alarm. Christiane's brown eyes were huge with anxiety.

"Of course we will, my darlings!" Mrs. van Maarsen cried, hoping to reassure them. "And I'm sure our new home will be very nice—you'll really like it."

The beautiful antique furniture that Jacqueline had seen every day of her life was removed and sold. Their new home was in the River Quarter, in another part of south Amsterdam, on Hunzestraat. It was a pleasant, busy neighborhood popular with Jewish refugees. There seemed to be more children too; on weekends and after school there were always girls and boys playing together on the grassy squares between the apartment blocks. Jacqueline remembers, "The house in the River Quarter was much smaller than the one we had before, and it must have been difficult for my parents, who were used to a certain luxurious sort of life, but I didn't care, even though I preferred our old house. I got a secondhand bicycle and rode it to school. There were hardly any cars then, apart from those belonging to the Nazis."

Despite these changes, life went on. Until the anti-Jewish laws took hold, Jacqueline went to The Hague to spend time with her cousin Meta, and she also saw a lot of another cousin, Deetje, who lived in Amsterdam. The three of them were about the same age and always found plenty to talk about when they were together. Jacqueline had always looked forward to Passover (a Jewish festival commemorating the Exodus of Jews from Egypt many centuries ago) because it meant that all the family would be together at Deetje's house, including Jacqueline's three Dutch uncles and their wives and children. She loved seder night (the first evening of Passover), when everyone sat down to tell the story of the flight from Egypt, then shared Deetje's mother's delicious homemade vegetable soup. After the meal, the adults would sing Hebrew songs whose very long refrains lulled the children to sleep.

In the last three or four years before the war, they were joined by David, Deetje's cousin, who was five years older than Jacqueline and attended a teacher-training college, where he was a brilliant student. Everyone loved David, and the girls thought he was great fun to be around. He was always smiling and loved to get a conversation going where everyone could join in, and he listened to the children as carefully as he listened to the adults. Everyone thought he had a great future ahead of him. He talked about going to Palestine to live and work, although the girls hoped he would stay in the Netherlands for as long as possible because they enjoyed his company. He always had a kind word and a joke to tell. He made every family gathering even more special, simply by being there.

In February 1941, the Nazi government announced that Jews of all ages had to register themselves. This way, the Nazis could find out exactly how many Jews lived in the Netherlands, where they were, and who they were. Jacqueline and Christiane's mother had four non-Jewish grandparents, but because their father was Jewish, they had to register too.

During those early months of the occupation, Jacqueline's biggest worry was the air raids. The warning sirens would emit their penetrating wail, and everyone dived for cover. This was particularly awful at night, since the silence of the sleeping city made all the noise seem louder and closer. Cone-shaped searchlights swept the sky, picking out the shapes of the German fighters and British bombers attacking each other. No lights were allowed anywhere after darkness fell, and special blackout boards or black curtains had to be placed at the windows of every house and building. The Nazis had set up a curfew, so no one was allowed out between the hours of midnight and four o'clock in the morning. Travel outside the Netherlands, at any time, was strictly forbidden.

Sometimes Jacqueline saw German soldiers on the streets, and often she passed NSBers (Dutch Nazis) strolling about as if they owned Amsterdam. She shuddered when she saw these men, most of whom had kept their political ideas to themselves until the German invasion. Now they wore their black uniforms with pride and jeered at Jews on the streets and in shops. Very often, gangs of NSBers would get on a crowded tram, haul out anyone who "looked" Jewish, and start hitting him. During one street fight between NSBers and Jews, a well-known Nazi was injured and later died from his wounds. In revenge, a large group of Nazis marched into the old Jewish Quarter and rounded up all the men and boys they could find, then beat them up before sending them away on trucks. No one knew where they had gone.

To her shock, Jacqueline learned that her cousin David had been among the men picked up by the Nazis that day. She was horror-struck: the thought of David, who had always been such fun, so kind, and who had lived life to the full, being harmed and taken from his family and friends was very hard to bear. A short while later, David's mother received a card informing her that he was on his way to a work camp in Germany. For weeks she heard nothing more. Then one day in spring, Deetje called for Jacqueline.

"I'm going to David's mother's house and wondered if you wanted to come too, to see how she is," Deetje said.

"Yes, I'll come," Jacqueline replied, and fetched her coat.

When they arrived at the house and opened the door, they were confronted with a terrible sight: David's mother was lying on the sofa, screaming and crying as though she would never stop. Deetje rushed into the kitchen to fetch a glass of water. Jacqueline saw a note on the table and read it in horror: David was dead. He had died in Mauthausen, a name that meant little to Jacqueline. Later she learned that Mauthausen was a concentration camp where Jews were worked hard and often beaten to death. Deetje tried to coax her aunt into drinking the water, but she carried on screaming. Jacqueline was unable to move, and stood staring at the grief-stricken woman. David, the boy with so much promise and good in him, was dead. The image of his devastated mother is something Jacqueline has never been able to forget.

There were people in the Netherlands who were appalled by the Germans' treatment of the Jews in the country, and at the end of February 1941, a strike was organized in Amsterdam and other major cities in protest at the deportations. For two days, trams remained in their depots; workers stood outside their offices, talking in the watery sunshine; and all the harbors and steel plants closed down. Furious, the Germans threatened to severely punish everyone involved in the strike unless it came to an end. There was no alternative but to go back to work.

Jacqueline had her first personal experience of anti-Semitism at a swimming pool that summer. Having decided that she would like to learn to dive, she joined a local swimming club. One afternoon, after Jacqueline had changed into her swimsuit and was waiting beside the pool with the other children taking lessons, the teacher came up and told them, "I'm very sorry, but those of you who are Jewish have to leave. You're not allowed into the water with the others." Jacqueline was stunned. What possible difference could being Jewish make in whether or not she was allowed to swim? It didn't make sense. Nonetheless, she felt embarrassed and humiliated.

She turned around and left the pool with the rest of the Jewish children.

The end of term came. It was Jacqueline's last at the Montessori school; she would be going to the Lyceum when the new term began, and she was excited about the prospect of attending "big" school. But one morning all the Jewish children were called into a meeting with the headmistress. Her words were almost an echo of what the swimming teacher had said: "Some of you are expecting to attend the Lyceum next term. I'm afraid that you are no longer welcome there, because you are Jewish children." Jacqueline shook her head in anger and disgust. The whole thing seemed so absurd—and cruel.

In the playground, she talked to two other Jewish girls who had also been excluded from their new school. Suddenly a group of boys approached them and began shoving them around, chanting quietly but viciously, "Jew-girls, Jew-girls, Jew-girls . . ." As the boys closed in, Jacqueline ducked her head and pushed through their hands. She ran and ran, through familiar streets that seemed unexpectedly menacing, and didn't stop until she arrived home on Hunzestraat, out of breath and dizzy.

She went to bed that night with the chants still ringing in her ears.

The shadow cast by the Nazi occupation grew longer with each passing day, and life for Jews in the Netherlands grew progressively harder as first one law, then another prevented them from doing their jobs and enjoying a social life outside their own restricted area. The non-Jewish Dutch population in general did little to defend the Jews, either out of fear for themselves or simply because they did not particularly care. As a result, Jews became more and more isolated.

Jacqueline spent most of the summer of 1941 with her friend Adrie. For six years they had played together and had been expecting to start at the Lyceum together in September, but the Nazis had put an end to that. Instead, Jacqueline and Adrie met up most days during July and August, knowing that they wouldn't be seeing as much of each other as they had hoped when the new school term began. Their favorite pastime was cycling in the countryside around Amsterdam. The flatness of the land meant that they could see for miles ahead. They chatted to each other as they pedaled, the sun warm on their faces and the breeze in their hair. They always brought books, food, and drinks with them on these days out, and they liked to find a pleasant spot to sit, read, or chat. The summer seemed to last longer than usual, due to the laziness of their days, but eventually it came to an end and Jacqueline prepared herself for her new school. She was a little bit nervous, but excited too, knowing she would make new friends there. At the very least, she could be certain she wouldn't be bullied on account of her Jewish father, since all the teachers as well as the pupils were Jewish. Even so, it made no sense to her that she had to attend the school: "We were not religious, after all. We only really went to synagogue for something special."

The new school was quite a long way from Jacqueline's home, and she had to bicycle beside the Amstel River to get there. The Jewish Lyceum stood on a street leading off the bank of the Amstel. There was a small playground in front of it and an archway where pupils would gather to chat while watching the boats chug down the river. Jacqueline's first day at the Jewish Lyceum was no different from that at any other school; she was told which was her classroom, listened as the teachers introduced themselves, then copied down timetables, and finished a bit earlier than usual.

Afterward, Jacqueline cycled home, pedaling quickly along the sunlit river and hoping that it wouldn't be too long before she made friends. Then she heard her name being called. "Hi, Jacqueline! Wait for me! Jacqueline! Wait!"

Jacqueline braked and turned around. A small, skinny girl with thick, shiny black hair was cycling energetically toward her. She stopped alongside Jacqueline and asked breathlessly, "Are you going that way too?" She pointed at the bridge over the river.

Jacqueline nodded and the girl smiled at her. She saw that the girl had braces on her teeth. "Great! Then we can bicycle home together from now on. I live on Merwedeplein."

Jacqueline knew Merwedeplein; it was a square close to where she lived in the River Quarter. She continued to gaze at this surprising girl, who suddenly realized that Jacqueline didn't know who she was.

The girl laughed and said, "We're in the same class at school. You didn't see me, did you?"

Jacqueline shook her head. "No, I didn't. What's your name?"

"Anne Frank," said the girl, pushing her thick black hair back from her face. Anne had long, sharp features and sparkling eyes with unusual flecks in them that made you want to look at them again. She began to pedal, although not as quickly as Jacqueline. "Listen, why don't you come home with me today? My parents won't mind. I've got an older sister too—

she's at our school, of course—her name's Margot. She's a little annoying, but not too bad really. My Oma [grandmother] lives with us as well—she came over from Aachen, to escape the Nazis. We're German, you see, or at least we used to be, but I don't like to say that I am now. I was born there though, in Frankfurt. We came to the Netherlands when I was four. That's a long time, isn't it? So I don't think I really qualify as German anymore, especially after what the Nazis have done to us. Do you?"

Jacqueline felt out of breath just listening to her new friend. Where on earth did she get her energy and confidence? Jacqueline had never met anyone like her. Before she could reply, Anne was off again: "Do you know anyone at this school? I know lots of girls and boys, but most of them aren't in my class. Which school did you go to before? I was at the Montessori school on Nierstraat. I had tons of friends there. And a boyfriend. Have you got a boyfriend?"

It was no time at all before they were at Merwedeplein. Jacqueline locked her bicycle to the railings and followed Anne up the steps to the first floor of the apartment block. Anne continued to chat as she fitted the key into the lock, opened the door, and then ran up another flight of stairs, leaving the front door to slam shut behind them.

Mrs. Frank was a solid-looking woman, sturdy rather than plump, with dark hair tied up in a neat bun, and large, warm brown eyes. Jacqueline could tell immediately from the way she welcomed her quietly that she was a kind woman but very reserved. Margot, Anne's slightly older sister, was attractive despite the thick glasses she wore, with the same abundant mass of dark hair as her mother and sister (although Margot's hair was cut in a shoulder-length bob) and her mother's expressive brown eyes. Margot smiled and said hello, then disappeared into her bedroom to do her homework.

Anne took Jacqueline aside, where her grandmother was sitting near the window, waiting to greet them and ask Anne about her day. The gray-haired old lady was very frail, but she listened with great interest to Anne's news. After talking to her grandmother, Anne led Jacqueline into the sitting room, where a huge window looked out over the square below. The room was very cozy, with lovely paintings on the walls, some pieces of fine sculpture, and lots of dark wood furnishings. A black cat slunk into the room and Anne picked him up deftly.

"This is Moortje," she said, "my cat."

Anne gave him a kiss and stroked his sleek back. Then she sat down in a large chair, placed the cat on the floor, propped her elbows on her knees, and looked at Jacqueline, with her chin cupped in her hands. "Now, tell me all about you," she said, with a wide smile.

The time passed quickly; Jacqueline found it easy to chat with her new friend, and whenever she ran out of things to say, Anne was always swift to carry on the conversation. While they were talking over glasses of lemonade brought in to them by Mrs. Frank, the door downstairs slammed again.

"That'll be Papa," Anne said, jumping to her feet eagerly. "He works in the city—he has his own business, selling spices and pectin."

"What's pectin?" Jacqueline asked.

"Stuff used to make jam and that sort of thing. Here he is."

Mr. Frank entered the room. He looked a little tired at first but smiled when he saw Anne and Jacqueline. He was a tall man and very slim, with a receding hairline and a thin mustache. "Hello there," he said, offering his hand to Jacqueline. His handshake was firm and friendly.

"Papa, this is Jacqueline van Maarsen." Anne's eyes danced as she introduced them. "She's at my new school and lives on Hunzestraat, near Miep. Do you know Miep Gies, Jacqueline?"

Jacqueline nodded. "Yes, of course—she and her husband, Jan, are our neighbors."

Anne smiled. "Really? Miep's worked as Papa's secretary since we got here—eight years! I went to her wedding this summer. It was *so* romantic."

Mr. Frank put an arm around his daughter. "So, how was your first day, Annele?" he asked.

"Tremendous!" Anne said enthusiastically, and launched into a long conversation with her father about the school, the teachers, the people she knew, and the boys she had seen in her class. Jacqueline listened to her with amusement. Clearly Anne was her father's daughter; they could both talk forever and were probably the most sociable people Jacqueline had ever met. When Jacqueline said that she had to return home, Anne invited her to stay for dinner, and after a quick telephone call to her mother, Jacqueline sat down with the Franks at their table.

Jacqueline enjoyed the dinner. Mrs. Frank said little, but a certain warmth came from her nonetheless, and there was some very sisterly bickering between Anne and Margot, which was broken up by Mr. Frank, laughing. Jacqueline was struck again by how similar Anne and her father were; both of them showed a deep interest in everything that was said and liked to hear everyone's point of view. Whenever

Jacqueline said something, she was aware of Mr. Frank's keen eyes regarding her, listening to her as few adults ever bothered to listen to children. He interrupted her only once, when she was talking about her family and explaining that her father was Jewish but her mother was not.

"Then why are you at the Jewish Lyceum?" Mr. Frank's brow was furrowed anxiously.

Jacqueline shrugged her shoulders. "Well, we had to register, of course, so we're regarded as Jewish by the Nazis."

Mr. Frank shook his head. "No, there's something not right about that. I'm going to speak to your parents about it." His dark eyes were serious and troubled. He said no more about it, but later, Jacqueline suspected he had done just that—and possibly helped to save her life.

After dinner, Jacqueline said good-bye to everyone and went outside with Anne, who stood leaning over the railing as Jacqueline unlocked her bike. "Thanks for a really nice evening," Jacqueline said, jumping on her bicycle.

"See you at school tomorrow," Anne said cheerfully.

"Yes, see you. Bye!" Jacqueline pedaled quickly to the main road. As she swung her bicycle across to the other side, she turned back to wave. She saw Anne wave too and then run up the steps. When she looked back again, Anne had gone. The sky was almost dark. The first stars of the evening glittered above the city's rooftops as Jacqueline rode home, smiling to herself.

Zonder deze kaart geen toegang.

——————————   ·

Wanneer men verhinderd is te komen,

gelieve tijdig te waarschuwen.

tel.90441

MRT 1942

rij II plaats2

Part of an invitation to attend a film show at Anne's house.

CHAPTER 3

GETTING TO KNOW
EACH OTHER

The following day, Jacqueline met up
with Anne again and realized that she liked her very
much. After a couple of days, Anne announced that
they were best friends and Jacqueline agreed, pleased
to have found close companionship so soon at her
new school. She and Anne shared the same interests,
particularly a love of reading. Their favorite author
was Cissy van Marxveldt, who wrote a series of books
about a girl named Joop ter Heul. Jacqueline and
Anne were as crazy about the books as children today
are about the Harry Potter series. The stories, then
very popular in the Netherlands, centered around the
imaginary heroine Joop from her school days until she
married and had children. Jacqueline and Anne talked
about the characters from the books almost as though
they were real people whom they actually knew, and

discussed the plot lines, trying to imagine what they would do in Joop's situation. They read many other books too; Jacqueline's father gave her a copy of *The Myths of Greece and Rome*, which Anne also really liked. She wanted it too, and asked for it as a present for her thirteenth birthday. When she wasn't given the book, she used the money she had been given to buy it. Jacqueline still has her own copy, safely put away in a cupboard.

The two of them also played endless games and almost wore out Jacqueline's Monopoly board. If they played at Anne's house, Margot would sometimes join them, and if they played at Jacqueline's house, Christiane occasionally took part. Through Anne, Jacqueline got to know Sanne Ledermann and Hanneli (Lies) Goslar. They all lived close to each other in the River Quarter. Together with Ilse Wagner, another girl from the Jewish Lyceum, they formed the table-tennis club, the Little Bear Minus 2. Ilse was one of the few people who never seemed to provoke Anne's irritation or good-natured teasing: everybody liked her sweet nature and sensible outlook. Sanne and Lies had been friends with Anne for years, ever since they all arrived in Amsterdam from Germany in 1933. Sanne was a very pretty girl, with clear blue eyes and a long black braid that hung all the way down her back. Her older sister,

Barbara, was a friend of Margot Frank. Lies was an easygoing girl, the only one of them who had a younger sister, Rachel (nicknamed Gabi), who was then two years old. Lies often had to help her mother look after Gabi and do some of the household chores. Her father and Sanne's father worked together in a business helping Jewish refugees with financial and legal matters.

Although they were all good friends, Anne didn't like Jacqueline to spend too much time alone with the other girls, because it made her feel insecure and jealous. Whenever Jacqueline went to someone else's house, Anne sulked about it afterward. "She considered that a betrayal of our friendship," Jacqueline recalls. The situation was even worse if Jacqueline visited a particular friend she had known before she met Anne. Jacqueline explains: "Anne was very jealous of her. We had been together at the Montessori school and then we were at the Jewish school again, so I had known her a long time. But in summer 1942 all Jews had to hand in their bicycles, and we lived too far from each other to go on being friends." Even when Jacqueline spent time with their mutual friend Ilse, Anne became jealous. She wrote in her diary, "Jacque has now become very taken with Ilse and behaves very childishly and stupidly towards me." The only other problem in their friendship was Jacqueline's occasional need to spend time by herself. Anne couldn't understand that, because she quickly became bored if she was alone.

Nonetheless, Anne was an ideal friend, and she and Jacqueline became very close. They were always happy to be in each other's company, talking, playing games, doing their homework together, or going through their postcard collections. Both girls had large numbers of colorful cards, and their favorites were photographs of movie stars. Anne had a vast collection of these, mostly featuring German actors and actresses, while Jacqueline preferred Hollywood stars. They loved the American teenage actress Deanna Durbin, whose films were usually a mixture of comedy and singing. Jacqueline also liked the child star Shirley Temple, as famous for her golden ringlets and dimpled smile as she was for her acting and singing talents. At first, Anne collected only postcards of film stars, but then she saw that Jacqueline had many postcards of well-known places, and she began to add these to the shoebox where she kept her collection. They sometimes swapped cards, and occasionally Jacqueline gave Anne some postcards she particularly liked.

Another common interest was fashion. Jacqueline's interest in beautiful clothes was probably sparked by her mother's background and work, but Anne was equally captivated by descriptions and illustrations of glamorous dresses, and she would wear only clothes that she really liked. Together they looked through magazines and the fashion pages of newspapers to discuss the latest clothes, and Jacqueline told Anne all about her mother's designs and customers. She showed Anne a clipping from an old newspaper mentioning a dress designed by Mrs. van Maarsen, which was described as "an enchanting gown of gold lace." Jacqueline told Anne how her mother had made the dress and insisted on having the color she wanted, despite the customer's preferring another color, and how her mother's choice had proved the right one. She and Anne frequently discussed the clothes they would wear after the war and which parties they would attend.

Postwar parties seemed such a long way off that Jacqueline and Anne decided to have their own. Anne was the principal hostess since she loved to organize people and be the center of attention, but Jacqueline had an equal hand in planning the parties, which were held at the Franks' apartment. Through their mutual love of cinema, the girls hit upon the idea of renting films and inviting their friends to watch them and have refreshments afterward. Jews could no longer attend public cinemas in Amsterdam, which meant that these events proved very popular with their friends and classmates. Back then, there were no videos or DVDs:

films were on large reels and a projector transferred the images onto a blank wall. Mr. Frank took the role of projectionist, while Mrs. Frank provided drinks and cakes for everyone who attended. Jacqueline and Anne pretended to be very strict about allowing in only "customers" who had tickets, but this was just because they enjoyed writing out proper invitations. Jacqueline still has one of their tickets; the yellowing slip of paper reads, "[Name] is invited on [date] with Anne Frank at Merwedeplein 37 at 11 o'clock to see a movie. Without this card, no entrance. Please inform in time. Row [number], Seat [number]."

Jacqueline and Anne were rarely apart, except at night and first thing in the morning. Jacqueline recalls, "Though we were together often, we almost never went to school together because I always ran late and preferred not to agree to come by and pick her up. The rest of the day, however, we were inseparable." After school, Jacqueline cycled with Anne back to Merwedeplein, where Anne would then go into the kitchen around four o'clock to make them something to eat, and to feed her cat. Later they would do their homework together in the sitting room. Jacqueline usually had to wait for Anne to finish her homework because Anne liked to do her best in each subject, while Jacqueline could hardly be bothered and did as little as possible to get by. "As a result," Jacqueline remembers, "I received some 'unsatisfactories,' while the diligent Anne excelled." The only subject Anne really struggled with was math, and she would leave this until last, then turn to Jacqueline and say, "Math, Jacque. Can you give me a hand with it? All these stupid figures mean nothing to me."

Frequently, Jacqueline would sleep at Anne's house or Anne would come over to hers. The day before Jacqueline's thirteenth birthday, in January 1942, Anne insisted on staying at Jacqueline's house. "Then I can be the first one to wish you happy birthday and give you a present," she explained. Anne loved to give presents as much as she liked to receive them, and was always happy to have something to celebrate. Jacqueline's family found Anne an entertaining companion to have around the house, and Mrs. van Maarsen in particular was amused by the way Anne always brought a suitcase with her containing curlers, hairbrush, and cape (to catch loose hairs during combing), as well as her pajamas. When Mrs. van Maarsen asked her why she was carrying a suitcase when she lived only a short walk away, Anne replied, "I don't feel like I'm really going away from home without it." On another occasion, the van Maarsens were just about to sit down for their main Sunday meal when Anne suddenly got up from the table and said good-bye.

Mrs. van Maarsen looked at her in surprise. "Anne, we're going to eat now."

Anne shook her head in response. "No, I have to go home. Moortje needs his bath."

With a laugh, Mrs. van Maarsen said, "Anne, that's crazy; a cat isn't supposed to be bathed!"

Anne gave her a hurt look and replied haughtily, "Why not? I've often bathed him and he's never said anything about it!" Then she fetched her suitcase and left.

Jacqueline's life was changed for the better by her friendship with Anne. She recalls, "Anne made everything fun. I have never met anyone else since then who enjoyed life as completely as my friend Anne did. It was always Anne who invented things to do together. Anne was the one with the movie-star collection, and I helped her with it. When we stayed at each other's house, it was Anne who decided about that. We alternated—not every night, of course, just sometimes—but Anne always invited herself. She decided what we would do, and I enjoyed it. She was pretty too. The photograph that everyone knows—where she sits at a desk with her arms folded—isn't her best picture. She had braces on her teeth then and was trying to hide it. She looked much nicer than that."

On March 23, 1942, Anne wrote in Jacqueline's poetry album. Most children in the Netherlands kept small autograph books in which friends would write a few lines of verse and then decorate what they had written with drawings or stickers. It was a tradition meant to provide the owner with happy memories of their youth in later years.

Anne wrote:

Amsterdam, March 23, 1942.

Dear Jackie,
Always show your sunny side,
And be a nice girl at school;
Remain my dearest little friend,
And everyone will love you.

In remembrance of your friend,
Anne Frank

At the time, what Anne had written was simply an expression of affection and friendship. Neither Jacqueline nor Anne could know that one day those lines would be reproduced in a special edition of her famous diary, to be read by millions of people, all over the world.

Anne Frank on the flat roof of her house
in Merwedeplein, 1940.

CHAPTER 4

SEPARATION

As the weather grew warmer that spring of 1942, Anne and Jacqueline spent hours sitting on "the terrace" at the Franks' apartment. They liked to set out two chairs on the gravel and talk while looking out over the houses and gardens between Merwedeplein and the main road. It became their special place, the spot where they told each other all kinds of secrets. Anne mentioned it later in her diary, when she wrote her farewell letters to Jacqueline after going into hiding, and told her to " . . . cut them up into tiny pieces, just like we did that time on the terrace with the note from Mummy's box."

Anne was referring to the time she and Jacqueline had taken a box of Mrs. Frank's tampons and read the instruction leaflet inside it. They were both curious about growing up, although Jacqueline was not as bothered about such things as Anne was, because her older sister, Christiane, had told her a lot already. Anne couldn't talk to her mother about anything like that; when she tried, Mrs. Frank replied firmly, "Anne, let me give you some advice: never mention the subject to boys and if they begin on it, then don't reply." Anne couldn't discuss such things with Margot, who she was sure would never even kiss a boy unless she was already engaged to him, so her sources of information were few.

"Daddy tells me bits and pieces," she explained to Jacqueline, but Jacqueline knew that Mr. Frank, although he was more open with his daughter than most parents of the time were, didn't tell her everything she wanted to know. Anne passed on what her father had said to Jacqueline, who had to laugh at the things Mr. Frank had come up with to stop his daughter from pestering him. She told Anne what she knew from Christiane, and was able to explain things in an easy, straightforward way. Anne later recorded in her diary how much better informed Jacqueline had been: "When I just turned 11, they [Mummy and Daddy] told me about having a period, but how it really came about or what it meant, I didn't find out until much later. When I was twelve and a half I heard some more, because Jacque is not nearly as stupid as I was. I had sensed myself what a man and a woman do when they are together; at first I was quite proud of my intuition! That it isn't the stomach that babies came from is something else I learned from Jacque, who said simply: 'The finished product comes out where it goes in!'"

Jacqueline knew that Anne was never satisfied with what she had learned: "She kept coming back with other stories she had wormed out of various people and to which she added her own fantasies. At the same time, she in turn felt the need to enlighten others, including the youngest boy in the class, with whom she had gone to primary school. This gave her the feeling of being grown up, which was very important to her." Anne showed Jacqueline how she had taken an old bra belonging to Margot and stuffed it with cotton wool to make her small breasts look bigger. Jacqueline giggled at this, especially because she didn't need to stuff her own bra. Anne was curious to know how Jacqueline's body was developing in relation to her own. When she stayed with Jacqueline one night, she did something that embarrassed Jacqueline very much: she asked Jacqueline whether they might feel each other's breasts. Shocked, Jacqueline said, "No! Certainly not!" Her face felt as if it were on fire. Before she could say anything else, Anne leaned over and kissed her on the cheek. Jacqueline was uncomfortable with Anne's behavior, but understood that she was just fascinated by what it meant to be growing up. Anne later wrote about the incident in her diary: "I remember one night when I slept with Jacque I could not contain myself, I was so curious to see her body, which she always kept hidden from me and which I had never seen. I asked Jacque whether as a proof of our friendship we might feel one another's breasts. Jacque refused. I also had a terrible desire to kiss Jacque and that I did." After that night, their friendship became easier for both of them; Anne realized now that Jacqueline needed more space than she did, and knew that she had to respect the difference in their personalities for the sake of their friendship.

One of Anne's favorite subjects that spring and summer of 1942 was boys. Jacqueline confided in Anne something that had happened to her the year before, when she and her friend Adrie had gone cycling. Adrie had gone off to pick flowers, and Jacqueline was sitting alone, reading, when two boys suddenly appeared. They were quite a bit older than she was and tall and strong, as Jacqueline discovered when they both leaped on her, trying to kiss her and pulling at her clothes. She managed to bite one of them and then Adrie came back. The sight of someone else frightened the boys off, and they ran away, cursing. Jacqueline realized she had had a lucky escape, but she regarded the boys as stupid idiots rather than a real threat. Anne recorded the attack in her diary while she was in hiding and in the middle of her love affair with Peter van Pels, the son of the family hiding with them: "Among other things I told [Peter van Pels] about the incident that had happened to Jacque and about how girls are completely defenseless when faced with such strong boys." The event had evidently made quite an impression on Anne.

Although she was only twelve, Anne was convinced that most of the boys she knew were in love with her! Jacqueline found Anne's vanity quite funny and tried not to laugh when Anne pointed out this or that boy, saying, "He's crazy about me—he looks at me all the time in class." Anne told Jacqueline about her first love, a boy named Peter Schiff, who had moved from Berlin to the River Quarter in July 1939 with his mother and stepfather. He and Anne had been close for a while, but he was three years older and eventually he decided Anne was too young for him. Anne compared all the boys whom she knew to him, and even declared that one day she would marry Peter.

Despite the war, this was a happy time for Jacqueline

and Anne. Although there were many anti-Jewish laws, the things that interested them most (board games, postcard collecting, home cinema clubs, and table tennis) were still available. Jacqueline later read an essay that Anne had written while in hiding, which brought the memory of that time vividly to life.

In "Do You Remember? Reminiscences of my School Days," Anne writes, "When we were still part of ordinary, everyday life, everything was just marvelous. That one year in the Lyceum was sheer bliss for me; the teachers, all that they taught me, the jokes, the prestige, the romances, and the adoring boys." In her diary she also mentioned one of her favorite places to hang out: Oasis, an ice-cream parlor in the neighborhood owned by a man from Berlin whose wife and daughter were Jewish though he was not. In the afternoons, all the adults would go there for coffee, and then afterward the place would fill up with schoolchildren and teenagers. The Little Bear Minus 2 Club never sat inside but instead bought their ice cream and stood outside to eat and see who else was around.

Jacqueline recalls, "We always ran into people we knew there. Anne loved walking behind boys and fantasizing that they were all her admirers. I didn't notice too much admiring going on, but they probably found her amusing, since she was cheerful and lively." After most table-tennis games, the Little Bear Minus 2 Club went to Oasis or to another ice-cream parlor nearby called Delphi. It was rare for them to have to buy their own ice cream; usually they met someone they knew who offered to buy it. Once they ran into Peter van Pels's father; he worked for Anne's father and was a loud, jolly man who told terrible jokes.

Frequently in their conversations, Jacqueline and Anne would talk about their home lives. Anne's beloved grandmother died of cancer in January 1942, after months of illness and an operation. Anne was deeply upset by her death and missed her support. Anne said often that she felt as though her family didn't take her seriously, especially since her older sister, Margot, was seen as the clever one and the "ideal daughter." Jacqueline listened to Anne's outbursts against her mother and her jealousy of Margot but tried to temper Anne's anger because she thought both Margot and Mrs. Frank were very patient and sweet with Anne. Jacqueline remembers, "Margot was always very nice to Anne. She really was the 'big sister.' I suppose I looked up to her, like my own sister. Margot was very intelligent, but I don't think I really noticed that then. I never saw any rivalry between them. Anne wasn't always nice to Margot, but she was never really horrible to her. I know there was one instance, though, when Anne was angry; it's one she mentions in her diary. Anne had been to the dentist and afterward Mrs. Frank and Margot decided to go shopping. They told Anne she had to go home because she had her bike with her. Anne came back afterward and she was furious that Margot went shopping while she had to come home. I have to say that I can't remember much about Mrs. Frank, because she was so quiet and never interfered. Mr. Frank would talk to us more and we would ask him things, so I have a clearer picture of him. Anne and her father were optimists and very outgoing, very friendly with everyone they met. There were no problems between them. Anne was a real daddy's girl!"

In spring 1942, during her visits to the Franks' apartment, Jacqueline noticed that their home was beginning to look different. At first she couldn't think what had changed exactly, but then one day she realized that all the chairs had gone from the living room and that there were older chairs around the dining table.

"Where have all your chairs gone?" she asked Mr. Frank, when he came into the room.

After a brief hesitation, he replied with a shrug of

his thin shoulders and a hearty laugh, "Oh, so you've noticed. We've sent them away to be reupholstered."

Jacqueline was puzzled by his reply. There were such horrific things happening every day that the adults she knew usually walked about with the weight of the world on them. Why on earth were the Franks worrying about their chairs? They had never struck Jacqueline as the type of people to bother about such things, especially since the chairs looked fine anyway. She said nothing more about it, even though the chairs never returned; but then other items disappeared from the apartment as well, giving the once cozy home a slightly neglected air. Perhaps they've sold their furniture, Jacqueline thought; perhaps they need the money. Where else could it have gone?

Jacqueline and Anne didn't talk much about the anti-Jewish laws. The laws were such a negative element in their lives, yet they got used to them very quickly. Adults seemed to find it far harder to cope with them, as far as Jacqueline could see. But gradually Jacqueline began to be aware of the danger that surrounded them all like invisible barbed wire. New anti-Jewish laws continued to be enforced on an almost daily basis. Signs bearing the words FORBIDDEN FOR JEWS appeared everywhere: parks, zoos, cafés, restaurants, hotels, theaters, cinemas, libraries, and

shops. Jacqueline once sat on a bench in Merwedeplein before realizing that she was not allowed to sit
there anymore. On another occasion she just stopped
herself from walking into a shop that wasn't for Jewish
customers. Her heart was beating loud and fast as she
turned away; something as simple and innocent as that
could have led to her arrest. It was no longer possible
to keep track of all these terrible laws because they affected everything.

In May 1942, the Nazis introduced a special badge
that all Jews had to wear. Jacqueline, Christiane, and
Mr. van Maarsen had to wear the large, six-pointed
yellow star, as did the Frank family, all the teachers and
children at Jacqueline's school, and many of her neighbors. The star made Jacqueline feel very vulnerable and
gave her the feeling that every German soldier and
Dutch Nazi in Amsterdam knew who she was. Whenever she passed a Nazi on the street now, she felt a huge
threat coming from him, as though her life was really
at risk. She knew she had to obey every law, because
the star let the Nazis know that she was Jewish and, as
such, someone whom they despised. It was a horrible
feeling, and Jacqueline told Anne, "I'm scared to do
anything, because everything is forbidden." Anne
recorded the comment in her diary, knowing exactly
what Jacqueline meant.

As May came to an end, Anne began to get excited about her birthday. She would be thirteen, which seemed very grown up to her. When the important day dawned, on Friday, June 12, Jacqueline met Anne at school together with the other members of the Little Bear Minus 2 Club. They gave Anne their joint present to her, a book called *Tales and Legends of the Netherlands*. Anne hugged the book to her chest. "Fantastic! This is just what I wanted!" They went along to their lessons; then at break time, Anne handed out some biscuits she and her mother had made. During PE, Anne was allowed to choose a game to play and suggested volleyball. Afterward, all her classmates linked arms and danced in a circle round her, singing "Long Shall She Live," the Dutch equivalent of "Happy Birthday to You." When that was over, there was a gymnastics lesson before Jacqueline, Anne, Lies, and Ilse walked back to Merwedeplein together.

When they arrived at the Franks' apartment, Sanne, the other member of the Little Bear Minus 2 Club, was waiting for them. Anne made drinks for everyone, then told them, "I got tons of presents, but I have to show you the best one. Wait there." She went to her bedroom, returning moments later with a very handsome book. It was thick, with white paper, and covered in a red-and-green checked material.

"It's a diary," Anne told them. "Papa bought it from the bookshop on the corner. I saw it, and said, 'That's the one.' Look, it even has a lock."

The girls murmured their admiration.

"I'm going to write in it every day," Anne said.

"What will you write?" Ilse asked, placing her empty glass on the sitting-room table.

"*Everything*. All my secrets and all my thoughts." Anne grinned. "And none of you will be able to read it!"

Jacqueline remembers, "It was her most important present. She would never know just how important it would become."

On the Sunday after her birthday, Anne's parents gave a party to celebrate their younger daughter's turning thirteen. Anne decided carefully whom she wanted to attend; Jacqueline remembers that the boys and girls present were the ones most in Anne's favor. When Jacqueline herself arrived, all the preparations for the afternoon were under way. Mr. Frank was checking that the projector worked properly so that they could watch a film, and Mrs. Frank and Margot were busy in the kitchen, while Anne rushed about excitedly. She was an excellent hostess, and stood by the door to welcome everyone who came to the party. An hour later, she had opened all her presents and the children were sitting together on chairs arranged in rows to watch the Rin Tin Tin movie *The Lighthouse by the Sea*. Lies had to leave the party early to help her mother with Gabi, but the others all stayed to enjoy the cakes and biscuits made by Anne's mother. When everyone had eventually gone, Anne and Jacqueline sorted through the gifts.

"Did you enjoy the party?" Anne asked anxiously.

Jacqueline laughed. "Of course! I think everyone else did too."

Anne nodded and smiled widely, her eyes sparkling with pleasure. "It was a great success, wasn't it?" she said.

Neither of them knew that it was the last birthday Anne would ever celebrate normally.

The summer holidays were fast approaching. Anne had been getting tutored after school in math. Jacqueline walked with Anne to the tutor's house and then waited for her so that they could return home together afterward. They talked constantly, and sometimes Jacqueline teased Anne over her new boyfriend, Hello Silberberg. He had been dating another girl when he met Anne, but dropped this girl to be with her. Hello was a German refugee who had arrived in Amsterdam a few years earlier and lived with his grandparents in the River Quarter. Hello's grandparents didn't approve of his relationship with Anne, but he continued to see her regardless. Hello was a handsome boy and very lively and outspoken. Anne wrote about him several times in her diary, but she was not in love with him: "My girlfriend Jacque teases me the whole time about Hello; I'm honestly not in love, oh no, surely I can have boyfriends. . . . " Jacqueline knew it wasn't anything serious; Hello was sixteen, but Anne was only thirteen—and she was still talking about marrying Peter Schiff one day!

The last weekend of June passed uneventfully. Jacqueline and another classmate spent Friday afternoon at Anne's house, baking cookies, which they then ate immediately. Jacqueline slept at the Franks' apartment on Saturday night and was with Anne most of Sunday. Later that day she went over to Lies's house and Anne wrote in her diary that she was "bored stiff." Jacqueline remembers that day very well: "I was sitting with Lies on her bed. Lies wasn't happy with Anne because Anne kept teasing her and being a bit unkind. I told Lies that Anne always wanted to know everything about me and could be a difficult friend. She was jealous and I had to belong to her alone, whereas I didn't mind if she met other girls. I remember it vividly, because afterward I felt so guilty that we had been talking about Anne behind her back. But she could be sure of me, because I wasn't attached to anyone else. I told Anne about the conversation with Lies later."

At the start of July, everyone's examination results were read out in the Jewish Theater. Jacqueline and Anne had done better than they had expected, and Margot Frank's report was outstanding. Anne was very proud of her sister for doing so well.

Sometime during the first week of July, Anne went over to visit Jacqueline's mother, to show off her new blue dress. Anne had just come in from the dressmaker when Jacqueline arrived. She was standing in the middle of the room, looking very pleased with her outfit and swinging from side to side. "Look, isn't it clever how the dressmaker lengthened the skirt? You can't see it at all," she said. Mrs. van Maarsen told her it looked wonderful. Jacqueline and Anne then chatted for a while, and before Anne went home, Jacqueline promised to call her on Sunday afternoon and arrange to do something together that day.

Sunday, July 5, 1942, turned out to be a brilliantly sunny day. It was quiet in Amsterdam; everyone seemed to be resting from the heat. Jacqueline didn't do much; it was just too hot to do anything except drink cold lemonade and try to stay in the shade. Shortly after three o'clock, she dialed Anne's number: 90441. She knew it well by now.

The receiver clicked as it was picked up: "Anne Frank."

"Hi, Anne, it's me."

"Jacqueline." There was a pause at the other end of the line, and a muffled voice in the background said something. When Anne spoke again, she sounded twitchy and unlike herself: "Listen, Jacque, I can't talk right now, I'm a bit busy. Can I call you back later?"

Jacqueline was puzzled. Was something wrong? She thought it better not to ask. "Yes, that's fine. Speak to you later."

"Good-bye, Jacqueline."

Jacqueline replaced the receiver and looked outside. The sun was still shining brightly. She could see it glinting on the windows of the house opposite.

As her thoughts drifted, a policeman appeared on the dusty street, stopping at the house opposite and ringing the doorbell. He handed a brown envelope to the woman who lived there and then continued on his way.

He must be sweating like mad in that horrible black uniform, Jacqueline thought idly. She saw the woman look down at the envelope for a long time before going inside again. There was something in her reaction that added to Jacqueline's sense of unease. I hope Anne rings soon, she said to herself quietly, and then went to lie down on her bed and read.

Anne did not return the phone call. Jacqueline never saw her again.

The Jewish Lyceum today, with a memorial over the entrance
to all the pupils who perished in the Holocaust.

CHAPTER 5

REMOVING
THE YELLOW STAR

Jacqueline woke up early the next day to the sound of rain falling steadily against her bedroom window. The weather had not quite broken; it was still very warm and only a storm would make it more bearable. She got out of bed and dressed slowly, wondering why Anne had not phoned back. I'll call her later, she thought.

Some time after breakfast, there was a knock at the door. Jacqueline went to answer it and found Lies standing there, her eyes huge with excitement. "Anne's gone!" she said in a high voice.

Jacqueline stared at her, then pulled her inside and closed the door. "What are you talking about? What do you mean, 'Anne's gone'?"

"She's run away to Switzerland."

"Alone?" Jacqueline could not believe it.

"No, of course not. With her family. Look." Lies grabbed Jacqueline by the sleeve, speaking in an urgent whisper. "This morning I went to get back the kitchen scale my mother had lent Mrs. Frank. When I got there, their lodger, Mr. Goldsmith, opened the door. He told me Anne wasn't there. He said that when he came downstairs this morning, he found a letter on the kitchen table asking him to take Anne's cat to the neighbors'. And there was a pound of meat for the cat as well. So he knew they weren't coming back for a while. Then my mother went to see if she could find out more, and Mr. Goldsmith told her he had found another letter addressed to someone in Maastricht. He called Mr. van Pels, who told him that Mr. Frank had a friend in Maastricht. This man probably helped the Franks get through Belgium and into Switzerland."

Jacqueline's mind reeled. She knew that Mr. Frank's mother and sister lived in Switzerland, which hadn't been invaded. It made sense for them to go there. That was probably the reason why Anne couldn't talk on the telephone yesterday, and why she hadn't called back: the Franks had been preparing to escape. It had to be true.

When Lies had gone, Jacqueline sat alone, her emotions in a whirl. She was very happy that Anne and her

family had been able to get away to an unoccupied
country where they could lead normal lives, but she
felt an overwhelming sense of loss and loneliness.
Still, she reasoned, the war couldn't last forever, and
they were bound to see each other again one day. This
thought cheered her up immensely. Then something
else occurred to her: had Anne left a letter for her, as
they had always promised each other they would in
these circumstances? She must have! Perhaps it was in
the box where she kept her movie-star postcards, or
somewhere in her bedroom. Jacqueline wanted to find
the letter, if there was one.

She called at Lies's apartment and suggested going
to the Franks' home together. Lies didn't expect to find
a letter for her from Anne, but she wanted something
that had belonged to Anne, as a keepsake.

The door was opened by Mr. Goldsmith.

Jacqueline smiled politely at him. "Would it be all
right if we came in, Mr. Goldsmith? We'd like to just
have one last look at Anne's apartment if we may."
Hoping to win his sympathy, she added, "We're really
going to miss her."

The middle-aged man shrugged his shoulders, and
Jacqueline and Lies climbed the stairs to the apartment.

They were unprepared for the sight that greeted
them. In the usually immaculate kitchen, the sink was

piled high with unwashed dishes and the breakfast things were still lying on the table. They walked into Anne's bedroom and stood silently for a moment, shocked by the knowledge that she had gone. Anne's bed was unmade, as if she had just left it.

Jacqueline looked down. "Anne's new shoes," she said softly. "She loved those shoes—she was really proud of them."

Lies said unsteadily, "Well, she'll be able to buy other ones, won't she? When they get to Switzerland, I mean."

Jacqueline didn't answer. An unmade bed was totally unlike Anne, and it seemed strange that she had left the shoes behind too.

Lies walked around the room, touching objects as if they might break. "Her diary isn't here. And she's taken her movie-star postcard collection."

"But not her games or books," Jacqueline said. On a shelf was Variété, a game Anne had received on her birthday and that she and Jacqueline had played again and again since then. Jacqueline was tempted to take it, but she knew that it was forbidden by the Germans to remove anything from a house that had been vacated by its Jewish inhabitants. She went farther into the room, looking for the letter she expected to find, but there wasn't one. Her head throbbed with worry as she thought about the situation. Why was everything in such a mess? Why hadn't Anne taken her new shoes? Why hadn't she left a letter?

"I'm taking these," Lies said suddenly, making Jacqueline jump; she had forgotten Lies was there. Lies was clutching Anne's swimming medals. "What are you going to have?"

Jacqueline felt lost. What she really wanted wasn't there. "Nothing," she said decisively. "I don't want anything. Let's leave—it doesn't seem right to be here without Anne."

They said good-bye to Mr. Goldsmith and then to each other. Jacqueline walked home deep in thought, hardly aware of the rain that still fell in large, warm drops from the clouded sky.

It was only after the war that Jacqueline learned the real reason for Anne's sudden disappearance, and the truth about where she had gone. On Monday, June 29, 1942, Dutch newspapers carried the story that all Jews were going to be sent to labor camps in Germany. During the first weekend in July, call-up notices had been sent out to thousands of Jews, ordering them to report to the SS. Most of those called up were German Jewish boys and girls about fifteen or sixteen years old, and among them was Margot Frank. Rather than let Margot report to the SS, the whole family had gone into hiding above the offices where Mr. Frank worked.

Returning to school after the summer holidays in 1942, Jacqueline noticed that many of the chairs in her class were empty, and each day when the register was read out, "Absent" was the reply given more and more often. The boy to whom Anne always aired her scant knowledge of sexuality was one of the first to go. Years later Jacqueline saw him again and learned that he, too, had gone into hiding. Another "absentee" was their friend Betty, whom Anne described in her diary as a sweet girl from a poor family. Jacqueline never saw Betty again, or most of the other children in her class. One of the teachers at the Jewish Lyceum later remembered how the older pupils developed a code to let him know whether the absent children had been picked up by the Nazis or had gone into hiding: "The children answered with gestures. There were two gestures: one meant caught; the other one, gone into hiding. Never a word was spoken during this ritual."

Every week, Jews were sent to the concentration camps in Germany and Poland from the Netherlands, just as they were from all the countries occupied by the Nazis. Some were sent call-up papers, but there were also mass "roundups." Jacqueline witnessed several of these: a street was sealed off and then trucks arrived, carrying groups of Nazis who leaped down and went from house to house, dragging out Jewish men, women, and children. It mattered little to the Germans whether the people they were taking were very young, old, pregnant, or sick; each and every one of them was forced into the trucks. Families were split up, grandparents beaten, rifles aimed at children to make them walk faster, and always these horrific scenes were accompanied by screams of abuse from the Nazi soldiers. The Dutch police took part in every raid, and eventually completely took over the task of rounding up Jews. They took advantage of the chaos to steal anything that could be carried: money, jewelry, food. The roundups made it clear that what the Nazis were aiming for was to rid the Netherlands of all its Jews. It was terrifying.

As a result of these roundups, Mr. and Mrs. van Maarsen became very protective of their daughters and always wanted to know exactly what they were doing and where they were when they were not at home. When Jacqueline told her parents that she wanted to see a performance by two famous Jewish cabaret artists (which only Jews were allowed to attend), they grew very anxious and at first told her she could not go.

Jacqueline understood their fears; the Germans often raided events like this one, but she desperately wanted to go and, in the end, her parents decided to allow it. Jacqueline herself was aware of the dangers, without realizing what the Nazis had planned: "When it came to the roundups, I didn't think anyone would be killed; I just thought that they would be made to do work. I never thought the Nazis would actually kill anyone I knew! You had no idea, really, because you had no previous experience to go on. Later on we heard that people were being gassed. Many people could not believe it, one of them being my father. But my mother did. She had a reliable source: my father's cousin, who was Jewish but was married to a German non-Jew whose brother-in-law worked in the Gestapo headquarters. He knew all about it."

At school the classes became smaller and smaller. Very soon, the teachers also began to vanish, either into hiding or as a result of the roundups. No one talked about the disappearances or asked any questions. It was too awful to discuss. Anyway, what was there to say? Nothing was going to improve the situation.

Not long after Anne disappeared, Mrs. van Maarsen decided to try to save the lives of her children before it was too late. Whereas Jacqueline's father could not bring himself to believe the rumors of the death camps, her mother was more aware of what was going on. Jacqueline explains, "She wouldn't allow herself to trust in false hopes. She decided to have my father's actions that made us Jewish children undone. The minute he found out, my father would have dug his heels in against it, so he wasn't allowed to know anything about it, and she forbade us to discuss it."

Mrs. van Maarsen had undergone a physical transformation too. After the Nazi invasion, she took to wearing an old bathrobe all day in order to save all her clothes for after the war. There were more important things than the beautiful clothes of haute couture in a world like the one in which they now lived, she thought. She took in mending, helped by a Jewish woman, to earn money, and for the first time she did all the housework herself, from the cooking and cleaning to the ironing. Their maid had gone, and Mrs. van Maarsen had no intention of allowing her daughters to ruin their soft young hands doing housework, although Jacqueline and Christiane wanted to help. Jacqueline admired her mother's attitude and had complete faith that if their future was in her hands, then everything would turn out fine.

Mrs. van Maarsen did not let them down, as

Jacqueline recalls: "One day she walked out of the door in full glory, perfectly dressed in carefully preserved clothes with a beautiful hat on her head. She went to the Gestapo headquarters in south Amsterdam. She told them that my father had made us members of the Jewish congregation without her knowledge and that she wanted to have that reversed. She made sure that she got to speak to someone higher up who also spoke French and, with the aid of her iron will and French charm, managed to convince him that he had to help her." The German officer told Mrs. van Maarsen that if she could produce birth certificates for her own grandparents, along with proof that they had been baptized, then he would see to it that Jacqueline and Christiane were taken off the Jewish register.

Although Mrs. van Maarsen was thrilled to have achieved so much with her visit into the lion's den, she then had to work out how she could get hold of the papers the Nazis requested. She contacted her brother in Paris, who was extremely worried about his sister and her family in Amsterdam, and asked him if he could help. He spoke to an uncle who was the manager of a famous restaurant in Paris, where he met many German officers. Through them he was able to have the necessary papers sent to the Gestapo headquarters in Amsterdam. Although Jacqueline and Christiane were soon to be no longer regarded as Jewish by the Nazis, Mrs. van Maarsen decided to make absolutely sure that they were as safe as they could be. She had grown up as a Catholic in France, but she had shown no interest in her religion since she was a teenager. In order to hoodwink the Nazis, however, she was determined that her once-Jewish children should become good Catholics. From then on, every week Jacqueline and Christiane visited the white church that dominated Amsterdam's Water-looplein square with its statue of Christ holding out his arms above the city. There they were given instruction in the Catholic faith by a priest and were presented with gilt-edged, leather-bound Bibles. Ironically, once Jacqueline and Christiane were finally taken off the register of Jews, they could no longer visit the Catholic church because it was in the Jewish Quarter, where only Jews were allowed!

In the meantime, Mr. van Maarsen discovered what his wife had done at the Gestapo headquarters. He was angry that she hadn't discussed the matter with him and upset that his children were not regarded as Jewish, but at the same time, he knew that their lives were no longer in danger. Mrs. van Maarsen had done an extraordinary thing; her actions meant that Jacqueline and Christiane were now able to live as "ordinary" children. The threat of being deported had gone, and the anti-Jewish laws did not apply to them anymore.

Nonetheless, Jacqueline's eyes remained open to the horrors taking place in Amsterdam. Sometimes Jacqueline's mother chatted to Miep and Jan Gies, who lived opposite them on Hunzestraat. Although Jacqueline knew that Miep was Mr. Frank's secretary, she had no idea, nor had Mrs. van Maarsen, that Miep was protecting Anne and her family and that she saw them every day. Jacqueline was never far from Anne's thoughts, and Miep often told Anne that she had seen Jacqueline and spoken to her mother.

Occasionally the members of the Little Bear Minus 2 Club met and talked about Anne. Everyone had heard the story about the Franks escaping to Switzerland.

"I hope she's happy," Ilse said, when they were all sitting together at her house.

"Of course she is," Sanne replied. "She's free now, isn't she?"

"I wish she was still here, though," Jacqueline said, "and that everything was normal again."

"No yellow stars for us either," said Lies.

"No roundups," Jacqueline said.

"No shopping in 'Jews Only' shops," Ilse put in.

"Being able to ride a bike again and go to the cinema." That was Sanne.

"Playing table tennis and then going to any ice-cream shop and not just the ones where Jews are allowed," Lies sighed.

"And having Anne back, swinging her hair about and telling us which boys are in love with her!" Jacqueline said with a smile.

They all laughed softly.

"At least she's safe," said Ilse.

Of course, what the girls did not know was that Anne was actually still in Amsterdam, missing them all and writing obsessively in the diary, which she called Kitty so that she would have a friend, even though it was only on paper.

Each of the Little Bear Minus 2 Club members was very different now from when they first formed the club. Part of that was due to their growing up, but Ilse, Lies, and Sanne were also terrified of being deported, while Jacqueline was learning to be a non-Jewish girl. She could now walk down the street without feeling a chill of fear whenever a German soldier passed by, and she was able to do all those things that she and her friends had discussed when they spoke about Anne living in Switzerland. The smallest things, such as being able to sit where she liked and walking through certain parks in the city, were now open to her again. She could take a tram whenever she wanted and go into any shop she liked, as well as go swimming and play games. Nonetheless, it felt strange to have such freedom when members of her family and her closest friends did not.

At the beginning of the Christmas holidays in 1942, both Jacqueline and Christiane were able to remove their stars. Mrs. van Maarsen carefully unpicked the yellow, six-pointed star bearing the word "Jew" from all their clothes. At first it was strange to walk around without the star after so many months with it, but Jacqueline quickly got used to it and was glad to wear clothes without it. As far as the Nazis were concerned, she was no longer Jewish, so the winter term of 1942 was Jacqueline's last at the Jewish Lyceum. In 1943 she would begin attending another, non-Jewish, school.

On her last day at the Jewish Lyceum, she stood and looked at the building for a long time. So much had happened during her year there. She had made new friends, and she had met Anne, her best friend ever. Then Anne had gone and the classrooms grew emptier and emptier by the day. The children and teachers who remained were quiet, subdued by the events taking place around them, which threatened to engulf them too. That terrible word "absent," which rang out time and again across the empty desks and chairs, had a completely different meaning now. There were hardly any pupils in the playground; no one wanted to hang around the school anymore. It felt safer at home, although for Jews nowhere was truly without danger.

Jacqueline turned away and began the long walk home alongside the river Amstel. As she came to the bridge where Anne had first called out to her, she stopped and looked out over the misty water toward the tower block at the end of Merwedeplein. It was almost dark, and within an hour everything would be plunged into blackness, as people closed the curtains across their windows, obeying the rule that said no light must show at night. There were few cars about and not many people either, only a sallow-faced, thin young NSBer who glanced at Jacqueline as he passed her. Jacqueline put her hands in her pockets and walked on, her head down against the winter air. There was no bright, laughing girl on a bicycle to accompany her now, only a damp mist and a bitter chill as the night descended.

Jacqueline (front right) with her sister and cousins
in The Hague, The Netherlands. Deetje is in the middle.

CHAPTER 6
LAST GOOD-BYES

As 1943 began, Jacqueline felt as though she was starting a new life. But it was not easy to make the change from Jewish girl to non-Jewish girl. She was nervous as she walked into her new school on her first day, feeling as though she wasn't supposed to be there. All the other girls reacted to her curiously too. She remembers, "It was as if I'd arrived from another planet. The anti-Jewish laws I had been forced to obey for the past two years left me with an inferiority complex, and I had trouble adjusting."

For the next few months, Jacqueline moved between two worlds: her days were spent in the non-Jewish school, where she couldn't get to know anyone at first, while in her free time she visited her Jewish friends. Since Anne's disappearance, Jacqueline had become close to Nanny Blitz, another pupil at the Jewish

Lyceum. At home alone she looked out of the window, seeing the neighborhood children playing. The girls played hopscotch and marbles, while the boys messed around on a patch of empty ground, building forts or playing football. Jacqueline noticed that two of them wore the yellow star on their coats. After a while, both boys disappeared.

In January, Jacqueline heard that Ilse Wagner, her friend and fellow member of the Little Bear Minus 2 Club, had been deported, together with her family. The thought of kind, smiling Ilse being loaded into a crowded train and driven to who-knows-where was too terrible to dwell on, but roundups in Jewish neighborhoods took place every day.

Jacqueline witnessed firsthand the scenes of brutality as Jewish families were hauled out of their homes and driven from the city. In horror, she watched the long lines of Jews walking through the streets with their backpacks and bags, hemmed in by German soldiers who tried to keep order by screaming abuse and aiming their guns at anyone who fell behind.

No one was supposed to watch the roundups, not even from inside their own homes, but Jacqueline would hide near the window and follow the appalling exodus with her eyes and heart. The anguished cries of those being deported rang in her ears long after the people themselves had gone.

She felt sick with anger at the way many Dutch people simply ignored the deportations, even when they happened right before their eyes. Most of the Netherlands' citizens continued their lives as normal, visiting the theater and the cinema and playing sports. One assembly point for Jews awaiting transport to Westerbork, the camp in the northeast of the Netherlands where they were kept before being sent to Germany and Poland, was close to a tennis court; those awaiting deportation could hear the gentle thud of the ball and the players calling to each other just a few feet from where they stood. Amsterdam was changing, growing smaller and meaner by the day as so many of its inhabitants departed for the nightmare journey eastward. One day the call-up came for Jacqueline's father, telling him to report to the SS, but the date kept being postponed due to Mrs. van Maarsen's visit to the Gestapo headquarters the year before. Nonetheless, Mr. van Maarsen's packed suitcase stood in the hall, in case the SS insisted on his deportation.

The Nazis didn't come for him, but other members of the van Maarsen family were not able to avoid the summons. In spring 1943, Jacqueline's cousin Deetje was deported, together with her parents. Shortly afterward, Jacqueline's youngest uncle in the Netherlands, who lived in Amsterdam, was also taken. At about the same time, her uncle and aunt who lived in the pretty town of Haarlem were deported as well. Jacqueline had heard nothing about them for some time, and when she asked her parents how they were, she was told that the Nazis had picked them up. Jacqueline was angry and hurt.

"Why didn't you tell me?" she asked, her throat tightening with the effort of trying not to cry. "You know how much they mean to me."

Jacqueline's father frowned and shook his head. "I'm sorry, Jackie, but we thought it was for the best. We didn't want to upset you—not with everything else that's been going on."

"I'm upset now!" Jacqueline responded, before leaving the room.

Today she remembers, "We spent so many holidays at their house, often with my aunt's nephews and nieces, during which time we were spoiled to our heart's content. My aunt had no children of her own. She never forgot our birthdays and her birthday cards are still part of my postcard collection."

In the space of a few short weeks, the van Maarsen family had lost several of its members, just as if they had evaporated into the air. Jacqueline visited her cousin Meta now as often as she could, wanting to be near those whom she loved while they were still around. Meta and her family had moved from The Hague to Amsterdam in 1942 because of a new law that said all Jews had to live in the Dutch capital. One day in March, when Jacqueline was visiting Meta with her parents and Christiane, she heard the news that she had been dreading.

When everyone was gathered together, Meta's mother said quietly, "We've got something to tell you." She paused as she looked at Mr. van Maarsen, who was her brother. "We've got to report to the Hollandse Schouwburg."

Jacqueline was stunned: everyone knew that the Hollandse Schouwburg was an old theater in the city used by the Germans to hold Jews awaiting deportation. There were rumors about the lack of air, food, and water in the building, about how anyone who tried to escape was shot; and that people had to sleep for days among the old seats and in the foyer, on the floor.

"All of you?" Mr. van Maarsen asked quietly.

Jacqueline's aunt nodded, her eyes welling with tears.

There was another silence and then Mrs. van Maarsen burst out, "But you'll be gassed! You mustn't go—you must go into hiding at once!" She grasped her sister-in-law's arm, insisting, "Don't go! Please, I beg you!"

Jacqueline stole a quick glance at her uncle, and could see from his face what he was thinking: that French woman always has to say something dramatic and upset everyone. His face went very red as he shouted, *"We're going and that's all there is to it!"* He put the cigarette he was smoking into an ashtray and ran a hand over his eyes, exasperated. "Besides, if we go into hiding and we're caught, then we'll get an S on our identity cards, and you know what that means."

Jacqueline did know; the S stood for *Straf* (punishment in German) and meant that when they arrived in the camps, their treatment would be worse than ever. She could also understand why her aunt and uncle were so terrified of doing anything that might anger the Germans; they were brokenhearted over the loss of their two older daughters, who had already been picked up. One had been taken away with her husband and baby, and the other had been deported with her husband of only a few days; she had married him quickly after receiving her call-up so that they could stay together.

Jacqueline's uncle stood up suddenly. "They're not going to get anything from us, though—I'll make sure of that." He picked up his cigarette and held it against the soft material of the sofa.

For a moment, everyone's surprise prevented them from speaking, but then Mr. van Maarsen grabbed the cigarette, saying, "Maurits, what on earth are you doing?"

Jacqueline's uncle glared back. "I told you, I don't want the Nazis getting their filthy hands on our things. That's why they want to get rid of us, isn't it? They're thieves, as well as thugs."

Jacqueline looked over at Meta, whose face was a picture of misery. She went to join her cousin and gave her a hug, noticing for the first time that the family's suitcases were in the hallway, awaiting their evening departure. When that time came, no amount of pleading would convince Meta's parents that it was better to stay and hide. Jacqueline stared at her father, who wept like a child when he took his sister into his arms for the last time. Jacqueline couldn't bear the sight of such anguish and, without another word or a backward glance, she rushed out of the door and ran through the dark, empty streets to her home, thinking all the time that she had lost yet more people whom she loved.

Jacqueline's circle of friends was now very small. She still saw Lies, Sanne, and Nanny, but hardly anyone else. Then she became friendly with a boy whose

parents knew her parents. He became Jacqueline's
first boyfriend, and she thought sadly how Anne
would have enjoyed teasing her about him, just as she
had teased Anne about Hello. Jacqueline's boyfriend
was Jewish. However, because his father was English,
his family believed that they had protection from the
deportations, so they were not in hiding. His family
and Jacqueline's spent Passover together in 1943, and
he presented her with a blue-and-white beaded bracelet at the seder ritual to mark the occasion. It was the
last time Jacqueline ever saw him. After a couple of
weeks had passed, she placed the pretty little bracelet
in a box, saying to herself, If I take good care of this
bracelet, he'll come back again. She hoped her wish
would work this time, remembering the clay doll she
had made, which now lay in the mud on the bottom
of a canal. But the boy never returned, and the only
reminder Jacqueline has of him is the bracelet still
lying in its box.

On June 20, 1943, Jacqueline lost yet another friend
in one of the biggest roundups of the war in the
Netherlands: fifty-five hundred people were picked up
in Amsterdam. Among them were Lies, her father, and
her sister, Gabi (Lies's mother had died tragically in
1942 while giving birth to a stillborn child). Jacqueline
didn't know what to do; it was awful to be so helpless

in the face of so much evil. The only people she had left, apart from her family, were Nanny and Sanne. Unfortunately, in September Nanny and her family were deported, and Sanne and her family were picked up on November 16. (Sanne's older sister, Barbara, managed to escape and went to work for the Dutch resistance, living under a non-Jewish name.)

Now Jacqueline had only her parents and sister left. In October, Mr. van Maarsen was finally allowed to remove the yellow star from his clothing. He had managed to get hold of a copy of a false statement saying that he was unable to have any more children, and this, together with his marriage to a Catholic, was enough to prevent him from being deported. He was the only member of his family to remain in the Netherlands; all his relatives, from the youngest to the oldest, had gone. Even his eldest brother had been deported, despite being married to a non-Jew. He had broken one of the anti-Jewish laws and that was enough for the Nazis to send him to his death.

After the last big roundup in September 1943, Amsterdam fell silent. The only Jews now in the city were those who had been sterilized so that they could have no more children, those few who were married to non-Jews, Jews with false identity papers, and those in hiding, such as the Frank family. The city felt completely different; it had lost its vibrancy and seemed to have no life left in it. The atmosphere in the streets was quiet and strained. The Germans were determined that even those Jews in hiding should be captured and deported, and they began offering a reward to anyone willing to betray them. Jacqueline hated those people whose desire for money was more important than anything else, and she was appalled by how many people were keen to earn the extra cash: "It soon became obvious to us that even those not sympathetic to the Nazi regime rather liked the idea." Jews found in their hiding places were immediately deported.

It was more than a year since Anne had disappeared, but Jacqueline was sure that she would see her again after the war. She missed her friendship and sense of fun. Jacqueline's new school was very different from the Jewish Lyceum; she had not been able to make any friends at all, which added to her sense of loneliness and not being part of anything. Much to her disappointment, Jacqueline failed her first-year exams there. This was not surprising, in view of all that had happened to her. Strangely enough, this turned out to be for the good: she was placed in another class, where she felt happier and made new friends. Although she liked these girls, Jacqueline never opened up to them: "I didn't talk about what had taken place in my neighborhood in the last two years. In fact, I wouldn't talk about it for a very long time." Jacqueline kept her feelings to herself.

Every time she passed by the local synagogue near their home, she paused and remembered how life had once been. There had been a time when the synagogue was packed with lively Jewish families spilling out onto the pavement and making plans for the future. Now the place was deserted and run-down. Jacqueline would stare up at the Hebrew letters on the gable—a silent testimony to the thousands of Jewish lives that had been completely swept away by a tidal wave of hatred.

Portrait of Jacqueline, age fourteen.

CHAPTER 7

THE HUNGER WINTER

As winter turned into spring, many people were hopeful that 1944 would be the year that the war ended. The Netherlands had been occupied for four long years, and it just didn't seem possible that another year could pass without the Germans being defeated. Everyone knew that the Allied armies were making good progress and that the Germans had lost tens of thousands of soldiers during the fighting in Russia. The Normandy landings on June 6, 1944, when 156,000 Allied soldiers landed in France on what became known as D-Day, filled everyone with fresh optimism. Those who had secretly kept their radios, even after the Nazis had forbidden them, listened obsessively to the news. Jacqueline remembers, "My family lived for the reports that struggled to get through to us and which slowly but surely grew more hopeful as far as the fighting was concerned. The faster the war was over, the greater the chance that family and friends would return from Germany, or so we thought."

At school, no one mentioned the war or the growing Dutch resistance movement. It was too dangerous: there were children whose parents were proud Nazi sympathizers, and there was also a teacher whom nobody trusted. To talk about the war in front of them would have been extremely foolish, since the Nazis arrested anyone who spoke ill of them. But people made small acts of defiance against the Germans: some teachers wouldn't teach from Nazi-approved textbooks, for instance.

Jacqueline's geography teacher was thought to be a member of a resistance group, but no one asked him outright whether this was true. When food became scarce in the winter of 1944–1945, he would always make sure that there was warm soup available at the school for all the pupils. Small acts like these meant a great deal in such times. Jacqueline had her own reasons to suspect that her geography teacher was involved with the resistance. One morning, on her way to school, she passed a couple of smoldering houses at a major crossroads where a German had been killed by the resistance. In revenge, the Nazis took some imprisoned members of the resistance out of jail and shot them on the spot where the German had been murdered. Then they set the two houses on fire and left the bodies of the executed resistance members on show to serve as an example to anyone who considered stepping out of line. Jacqueline knew that her geography teacher had to pass by the burning houses and bodies on his way to school. When she saw him later that day, she noticed that he was shaking and unable to give the lesson in his usual efficient way.

Although the city seemed much quieter than before, there were incidents that reminded Jacqueline that the Germans were still eager to hunt down any Jews who had avoided the deportations. Twice, a distant relative of the van Maarsens arrived unexpectedly at their home in utter panic. He had been in hiding, but the Nazis were after him and he had been forced to move on. On both occasions Jacqueline's parents covered for him until he felt able to go outside again and find another hiding place. Jacqueline hardly knew him at all, and stood in the corner of the hall, staring at him with a mixture of horror and pity as he sat listening to every footstep with terrified eyes. Jacqueline was frightened too, for the Germans were still in the habit of doing house-to-house searches for Jews. What if they knocked at the door or broke it down? They could do so quite easily, and at any moment. If they found the fugitive, then they would arrest the whole family. Jacqueline was a bundle of nerves until the relative had gone.

There was another, more constant, fear in Jacqueline's life then: the possibility of being bombed. Allied aircraft flew over Amsterdam every night on their way to bombing missions in German cities, and there were frequent dogfights in the sky between Allied and German pilots. In the River Quarter, people would stand in the archways between the apartments, watching the planes drone over. Search-light beams scanned the sky and the antiaircraft guns boomed and flashed. Few bombs actually fell on Amsterdam, but the noise of the firing from the airplanes high above was deafening. Houses appeared to shake under the ferocious attacks, and there was no real protection from a bomb or falling aircraft. Once, a British airplane crashed in the center of the city; some buildings were destroyed but, incredibly, no one was injured. Jacqueline covered her ears whenever the fighting in the sky began and tried to sleep, even though she knew it was impossible in the middle of such uproar.

As summer 1944 came to a close, Allied soldiers reached Maastricht, a Dutch city close to the German border. Its inhabitants were now free of the Germans, and invasion fever gripped the country. Many people were sure that the complete liberation of the Netherlands was close at hand. On Tuesday, September 5, rumors that the Allied soldiers were on their way were so convincing that people in Amsterdam began hanging out flags and waving anything orange (in honor of the Dutch royal family, who was known as the House of Orange). Large crowds gathered on the streets to welcome the liberators, and most NSBers fled, followed by many German troops. By daybreak on September 6 it was obvious that the whole thing had been a big mistake and the Germans had left to fight the Allies outside Amsterdam. The day became known as Dolle Dinsdag (Mad Tuesday). All was not lost, however; later that month thousands of Allied parachutists landed near Arnhem, and the south of the Netherlands was liberated. Unfortunately, the west remained under Nazi control.

Although during the war food had been distributed according to a coupon system, rations began to be cut as supplies grew smaller. Sometimes Jacqueline went with her mother to wait in line for groceries, coupons in hand, only to be told that there was nothing left when they reached the counter.

"You must have something for us," Mrs. van Maarsen would say, but the shopkeeper just shook his head.

"Nothing at all?" Jacqueline would ask.

"Nothing at all," he replied.

They would walk to another shop, and another, and another, only to hear the same thing: "I'm sorry, but you're too late. Stocks are gone."

The Netherlands was entering a period that would later become known as the Hunger Winter. Large lines of people, stamping their feet in the cold and blowing on their hands for warmth, started to form outside shops in the early hours of the morning. Yet only the first few people in the line could expect to receive anything, and what they were able to buy was pitiful: a single bread roll, which had to last a family several days.

When Jacqueline walked to school, she saw old people slumped in doorways, too tired to walk any farther, their legs swollen because they were starving to death. The young and the very old were most at risk, and with this in mind, leftovers from the kitchens of the German army were put aside for schoolchildren, and one school distributed them. Jacqueline went there sometimes and ate everything she was given, except one kind of soup, made from potato peels, which made her stomach churn. People were eating all sorts of things—tulip bulbs, sugar beets, and even candle fat—in their efforts to get rid of the hunger pangs. Some traveled to the countryside to buy or barter food from farmers, who took linen, soap, and matches in return for eggs and milk. But most people couldn't do that and had to be content with whatever they could find in Amsterdam.

Then, just as it seemed things could not get any worse, the Netherlands' railway workers went on strike on the orders of the Dutch government in exile in London. As punishment, the Germans cut off food and electricity supplies. The trams in Amsterdam stopped running, and coal couldn't reach the city, so there was no fuel, no light, and no warmth. Jacqueline's mother took to cooking on a tiny emergency burner, but it didn't heat the room. As winter drew on, Jacqueline went to bed very early, wearing as many clothes as possible so that she could sleep and forget the cold and her empty stomach.

During the past year, despite all the hardship, Jacqueline's confidence had returned. She now had a circle of friends again and was a member of a hockey club and a tennis club. She liked all these new elements in her life, but missed her friends from the Little Bear

Minus 2 Club very much. None of her new friends was Jewish. One of the girls in her hockey club was Corrie Kleiman, whose father, Johannes, worked as a bookkeeper for Mr. Frank's old company. Mr. Kleiman was one of the group of four office workers, including Jacqueline's neighbor Miep Gies, who was secretly taking care of the Franks in their hiding place. But Jacqueline had no idea, and neither did Corrie, who had not been told her father's secret.

A boy named Thijs developed a crush on Jacqueline and asked if he could walk her home one evening. When they arrived at Jacqueline's apartment, she invited him in. It was the middle of the Hunger Winter, and Mrs. van Maarsen was scooping some dried beans out of a sack; every week she cooked some of them to make a meal for the family. Suddenly Jacqueline noticed a married couple who were related to cousin Deetje sitting in a corner of the room. Although the couple were in hiding, they ate at the van Maarsens' home occasionally because their hiding place was without food and heat. They always sat near the tiny burner to try to get warm before leaving again for their cold, dark, and utterly miserable hiding place. Sometimes Jacqueline saw them sneak a bean out of the pan, but she never said anything because she knew that they were literally starving to death. Their situation was hopeless, and the time they spent in the van Maarsens' house was the only way they were able to get through the days and nights that stretched ahead of them.

Jacqueline felt a prickle of fear at the sight of the couple; she had no idea how she could explain their suspicious presence to Thijs. She saw him look at the two people huddled together in the semidark corner. Thijs frowned slightly, as though trying to work out for himself who they could be, and why they looked so thin and miserable. He nudged Jacqueline. "Are they Jews?"

Jacqueline's mind raced. What should she say? She didn't want to lie, but she didn't trust Thijs either. "No," she whispered back, shooting a glance at Thijs. "They're just friends of my parents who're hungry, that's all."

It was perfectly obvious from his unfriendly stare that he didn't believe her. The couple didn't move and Jacqueline wondered if they had heard what was said.

Later that evening they left, and Jacqueline never saw them again. It was the last time she was alone with Thijs too; when she asked him a few days afterward why he seemed to be avoiding her, he answered with a curl of his lip, "I don't want anything to do with Jews." That made everything simple for Jacqueline too; if that was how he felt, then she didn't want anything to do with him either.

By the end of 1944, those areas of the Netherlands that had not yet been liberated were at a standstill. Businesses closed down; telephones no longer worked; there was no mail, no garbage collection, and the sewers began to overflow, resulting in a spreading plague of rats and disease. The problem of starvation in the cities had reached crisis point, with more than five hundred people a week dying of hunger in Amsterdam alone. There was no wood available for coffins because it had all been used for fuel, so the dead were buried wrapped in paper or bedsheets. As spring began, the number of deaths in the Netherlands due to starvation, disease, and the effects of the bitterly cold winter amounted to more than twenty thousand. When news of the situation reached Great Britain, Royal Air Force (RAF) planes began to drop food over Amsterdam. For the past few years, Jacqueline had been terrified by the sound of aircraft, but now she jumped for joy, knowing that they were bringing much-needed supplies to a starving population.

Jacqueline was at school when the first lot of food parcels arrived. It was April 29, 1945. She was sitting quietly, reading from a textbook and trying to ignore her rumbling tummy and aching head, when she heard a low drone outside. One of her classmates rushed over to the window, looked out at the clear sky, and then turned around in great excitement. "It's the British! They're dropping food!" Everyone jumped to his or her feet, shouting with joy. The teacher flung open the door with a cry of "Hurry! Hurry!" and hustled everyone out and up the stairwell.

The group of girls clattered up the steps, chattering and laughing. When they reached the roof, they began racing about, waving anything they could find: shawls, handkerchiefs, even their cardigans.

"They're here! They're here!" one of Jacqueline's classmates sang. To them, the planes were symbols of freedom and friendship, as trusted and welcome as the Germans were feared and hated.

Objects began dropping from the clouds. Jacqueline could see other people now, gathering on the roofs of nearby houses, shouting to each other, laughing and crying all at once. It was as though the whole of Amsterdam had rushed to their rooftops and were waving in delight at the sturdy planes gliding gracefully overhead. Every now and then the Lancaster bombers would dip a little, doors on the underside of their metal bodies would open, and then small parcels or crates of food would be hurled out. When all the supplies had been delivered, the planes' crews began throwing out what was in their pockets: chocolate and cigarettes, mostly. Jacqueline was waving both arms madly, tears of delight streaming down her face, when she happened to glance at the other side of the canal, where a large house served as a base for a group of German soldiers. She could see their angry, contorted faces through the windows, their uniforms neat and clean, their bodies well fed. And then they disappeared.

Suddenly the headmistress appeared. "Everybody down from the roof. Quickly now, no dawdling," she said, her face puckered with anxiety.

Jacqueline guessed what had happened: the Germans had stormed over and ordered the headmistress to retrieve her pupils, unable to stand the sight of them cheering the British planes. What cowards they were, Jacqueline thought; cowards and vengeful, hate-filled men.

In the end, those German soldiers' victory was short lived. The RAF had dropped hundreds of food parcels over Amsterdam that day, and they came back, again and again. By then people were waiting with banners that had messages written in thick black letters. Most said WELCOME or THANK YOU, but a few even said CIGA-RETTES, PLEASE! The Americans joined in on May 1, and white parachutes dropped out of their B-17 bombers, with the food tied up in boxes or crates. The flour that fell from the sky went to Amsterdam's bakers to make bread, while everyone got a share of what was in the other parcels. Hungrily, Jacqueline ate the "Swedish white bread," smeared with margarine, that had fallen from the clouds, certain that she would never taste anything as delicious ever again.

Anne at school, 1940.

CHAPTER 8

LIBERATION

On May 5, 1945, Amsterdam was liberated by Canadian soldiers. Three days later the German Army capitulated and the war in Europe was officially over. For years people had been walking around in old, worn-out clothes, and the last few months had passed by in a gray haze of misery. To Jacqueline, news of the liberation and the German surrender filled the world again with a child's paintbox of brilliant color. Everything seemed to sparkle, looking new and bright, and the days were suddenly filled with sunshine and blue skies. It was like waking up from a dark nightmare.

When the news spread around the River Quarter that the Canadian soldiers would be passing through their neighborhood, everyone—young and old— began spilling out of the houses and running down the streets toward the bridge over the Amstel River that their liberators would cross. This was near where Jacqueline had first met Anne, a lifetime ago, or so it seemed. Jacqueline thought excitedly about hearing from Anne again; perhaps the Frank family would move back to Amsterdam now that the war was over. They would renew their friendship—what a lot they had to tell each other! But would Lies, Sanne, Ilse, Nanny, and all the other children who had disappeared return? Would life be as wonderful again as it was before? At the time of the liberation, Jacqueline was still hopeful.

As the sun shone down on Amsterdam, through the mass of cheering people Jacqueline saw the grinning, gum-chewing Canadian soldiers sitting on top of their green tanks and trucks. They looked young, handsome, happy, and well cared for—like the movie stars on the postcards Jacqueline used to collect. One of the Canadians leaned down and offered Jacqueline his hand. She took it and jumped up onto the truck, breathless with excitement. Hundreds of people—girls especially!—were doing the same. The sky was filled with shouting and singing and laughter. The Dutch flag waved from hundreds of windows as the Canadian convoy passed slowly by, unable to proceed at anything more than a snail's pace because everyone wanted to shake hands with the soldiers, or clap them on the shoulder, or give them a kiss. The trucks and tanks rolled on to the big park close to where Jacqueline had lived as a little girl. The wheels crunched over the gravel and left tire marks in the grass. More people were waiting to greet their liberators, adding to the crush of well-wishers who had trailed after the vehicles.

In the park, the soldiers climbed down from their trucks and tanks and began pitching tents. They handed out tins of meat and vegetables, chocolate, gummy candy, and cigarettes to the crowd. Jacqueline gazed down at the chocolate bar she had been given. She hardly recognized it; years had gone by since she had last eaten chocolate. She tore off the paper wrapping and bit into the bar, then closed her eyes as it melted in her mouth: what heaven! She stayed to watch the Canadians make their final preparations for the night before joining the crowds who waved farewell to the soldiers and began the long walk home. There was no public transportation, but nobody minded at all. The walk was more fun than Jacqueline had had in years: lots of singing and laughing, dancing, and eating chocolate. Everyone was eating chocolate!

When Jacqueline woke up the next day, her first thought was: we're free! Her whole body felt light with happiness. She refused to think about the past and the possibility that the future might not be everything she hoped it would be. Nothing is going to spoil this feeling, she thought determinedly. I'm going to enjoy myself for a change.

Outside, people were smiling again and looked more relaxed than they had for as long as Jacqueline could remember. Even the pigeons, which had disappeared during the Hunger Winter because there was no food for them either, had returned and were settling on the orange rooftops in cooing, fluttering circles. At school, everyone learned the Canadian national anthem and sang it again and again.

Although the Allies had arrived, there were still some Germans in Amsterdam. In the afternoon of the first day following the liberation, one of Jacqueline's neighbors placed his radio on a windowsill so that the amazing news of Europe emerging from the Nazi shadow could be heard in the street. Jacqueline joined the large crowd who gathered to listen. Suddenly a group of German soldiers appeared. Silently, they lifted their guns to their shoulders, preparing to fire. For a moment, nobody moved, then everyone started screaming and running. Jacqueline fled as fast as her feet would carry her, and she was almost sick when she reached home, slamming the door behind her. Later, she learned that some Germans had opened fire on people celebrating the liberation in the city center. Twenty-two had been killed, including a member of Jacqueline's hockey club. She felt numb upon hearing the news; would the Germans never leave them alone, never stop terrorizing them? But eventually they did. Those who weren't able to escape from the Netherlands were arrested, along with the Dutch people who had collaborated with them. They were placed in prisons and camps, awaiting trial.

It wasn't long before the street parties began. Committees were set up in every neighborhood to organize all manner of events. During the day there were games and tables laid out with food for people to enjoy. At night the squares were hung with lights, and music was played at tremendous volume. Jacqueline and a group of her friends went from party to party, dancing all through the night to fast American music. Everyone wanted to forget the past for a while and just enjoy the sensation of being alive and free.

The parties could not go on forever, though, and eventually people had to begin rebuilding their lives and trying to find out what had happened to those who had been deported.

Jacqueline waited anxiously for her family and friends to come back. She looked forward to welcoming them and to supporting and helping them in any

way she could. On May 5th, she had seen one of the
two boys with a yellow star who had played in her street
during the war. She found out that he and his parents
had been in hiding for two years in an attic in a neighbor's house. It was some months before she saw the
other boy again. In the meantime the survivors of the
concentration camps began to return. These people
came back to the Netherlands like people from another
world. They had lost everything—homes, jobs, and
families—and their bodies and minds might never re-
cover.

The summer of 1945 was filled with newspaper reports of what had happened in the camps. Photographs
of thousands of diseased, starved bodies piled up in
open mass graves were printed, along with eyewitness
accounts from the first Allied personnel to arrive at the
camps. The rumors about the gas chambers—too terrible to believe at the time—proved to be true.
Jacqueline was shocked to the depths of her soul by
what she read and saw.

One day a girl came to her home. Mr. van Maarsen
had known her father before the war. She had been in
Auschwitz and all her family had been killed. She knew
no one else in Amsterdam and fell against Mrs. van
Maarsen, sobbing hysterically. Jacqueline looked at the
girl's stick-thin arms; on one was a crude black tattoo

of numbers. The girl caught Jacqueline's gaze and wiped away her tears to explain, "That was the number they gave me in Auschwitz. Nobody had names there— we were just numbers to the Nazis." The girl stayed up all night talking to Mr. and Mrs. van Maarsen, while Jacqueline and Christiane were sent to bed early. Jacqueline lay in her room, staring at the ceiling. The evening was no longer torn apart by the sound of dog- fights in the sky between the Allies and the Germans. She had listened night after night to the sound of the guns, but now all she could hear was the low murmur of voices in the sitting room as the girl poured out her experiences in the Auschwitz camp.

Jacqueline soon realized that life was never going to be the same again. The Red Cross published lists of those who had died. Within weeks it was obvious from the empty houses, silent schools, subdued work- places, and quiet streets that most of those who had been sent to the camps had been killed. Those few who did come back looked like ghosts, and the sto- ries they told about how their families and friends had died were almost unbearable to hear. Hardly anyone Jacqueline knew returned from the camps. None of her family returned, and most of her former classmates at the Jewish Lyceum remained forever "absent." Almost all the teachers from the school had died, but those who did survive went back to teaching again. One of them, history teacher Jacques Presser, would eventually write the best-known account of the Jewish deportations: *Ashes in the Wind: The Destruction of Dutch Jewry*. Anne's great love, Peter Schiff, had been murdered in Auschwitz, although it was not known for certain when he died. Two former members of the Little Bear Minus 2 Club did not come back: Sanne and her parents were gassed in Auschwitz only hours after arriving there, and Ilse and her parents suffered the same horrific fate in Sobibor.

One day, Jacqueline had an unexpected visitor. The knock on the van Maarsens' door came in June 1945. Standing there in a suit that hung from his gaunt frame was Anne's father.

"Hello, Jacqueline," he said softly. His eyes were deeply sad.

For a moment, Jacqueline said nothing, shocked by his sudden appearance. Then she regained her composure and invited him in. He walked through to the sitting room while Jacqueline brought him a drink. And then, very slowly and in a voice so low that she had to lean forwards to hear what he said, Mr. Frank told her what had happened to his family.

He explained that they had never really gone to Switzerland at all, but had been hiding in the annex above his workplace. For two years, together with the van Pels family and a dentist friend named Pfeffer, they had remained safe, looked after by four of Mr. Frank's employees, including Jacqueline's neighbor Miep Gies, whose husband also provided them with extra ration cards. In August 1944 they had been betrayed and were sent to Westerbork to await their deportation.

Mr. Frank said with a crooked smile, "You know, Anne was almost happy there. It might sound unbelievable but at least she could feel the sun on her face again and was able to make a few friends. After two years in hiding, it was a sort of freedom. The roll-calls, the filth, and the humiliation of being there—that was hard, you have no idea how hard, but we could put up with it because we didn't think we were going to be sent on. We thought it was only a matter of time before the Allies reached us, and we really believed we could remain there long enough to see the liberation. But then we were put on the deportation list. . . ." His smile faded and he swallowed hard. "We ended up on the last train to Poland. The last one."

A haunted, hunted look crept over Mr. Frank's skeletal face. In a very soft voice, he told Jacqueline that they had been sent to Auschwitz, traveling for three days and nights in locked, overcrowded cattle cars with almost nothing to eat or drink. Many had died on the journey. When they arrived in Auschwitz, families were split up: men had to go to one part of the camp and women and children to another. "It was the last time I saw my wife and Margot and Anne. I saw Margot's face as they were dragged away. . . . " He paused. "The look in her eyes will stay with me forever."

Mr. van Pels was sent to the gas chambers in Auschwitz. In December 1944, Mr. Pfeffer was transferred to another camp, where he died. Mr. Frank ended up in the hospital in Auschwitz, after a terrible beating by one of the camp guards. Peter van Pels, with whom Anne had fallen in love while they were all in hiding, brought him food every day and kept him alive. Then, in January 1945, as the Allied liberators closed in, the SS started to destroy Auschwitz and to force everyone who could still walk on a "death march," away from the evidence of the horrors. Peter was taken on one of the marches and died in another camp. The Russians liberated Auschwitz a few days later, and Mr. Frank was there, half alive, when they came.

Jacqueline said nothing; what was there to say? Mr. Frank took out his handkerchief and dabbed at his eyes. "My wife, Edith, died in Auschwitz in January 1945. She starved to death. But the children . . . " He took a deep breath and said more steadily, "Margot and Anne were sent to another camp in October. That's all I know. But they were young and strong, and I am sure . . . I feel certain—"

"That they are alive," Jacqueline finished for him. She wanted to offer him hope, but in the past few weeks she had seen her own father devastated time and time again after reading the Red Cross lists of the survivors and the victims. Cousins Deetje and Meta had been on one of those lists; they were never coming home. And they had been young and strong as well, just like Margot and Anne Frank. If Deetje and Meta hadn't been able to survive, what reason was there to hope that Margot and Anne had? But Jacqueline kept these painful thoughts to herself and promised Mr. Frank that if she heard anything about his daughters, she would contact him immediately.

"We're neighbors," he told her. "I'm living with Miep and Jan Gies for now." The haunted look returned to his eyes as he said, "I have nowhere else to go."

Mr. Frank visited quite often after that, but at the end of July 1945, he came with news about his children. Jacqueline knew immediately what he was going to say. His welling eyes and the way his whole body trembled with grief told her all she needed to know. Jacqueline led him toward a chair, and as he lowered himself into it, he began to cry. Between wrenching sobs, he said that he had found a nurse who had known Anne and Margot in the Bergen-Belsen camp, where they were sent from Auschwitz. Although Belsen had no gas chambers, hundreds of thousands of people died there from starvation and disease. Survivors said that it had been the worst camp of them all. Margot and Anne caught typhus, a deadly disease that claimed many lives in Bergen-Belsen. In March Margot died while trying to get out of her bunk. She fell onto the cold floor of the barracks and, because she was so weak, the shock killed her. During the next few days, the nurse and her sister tried to care for Anne, who was so horrified by the lice in her clothes that she walked around with only a blanket to cover her—in the middle of winter. No one told her that Margot was dead, but after a few days Anne sensed it for herself. Anne had already told people that she felt certain both her parents were dead, and now the loss of Margot broke her spirit. She died in Bergen-Belsen at the age of fifteen. Three weeks later, British troops liberated the camp.

Why, why, why? Jacqueline wanted to scream. Why had this been allowed to happen? She felt as though she had been hit. Her throat closed up and her limbs became stiff. The thought of Anne—bright, lively, laughing Anne, the young girl with sparkling eyes who was always such fun—dying in misery and alone, her body broken by typhus and starvation, made Jacqueline feel as though nothing would ever be right again. Anne had done no one any harm and she had so much to offer the world. She might have got married and had children of her own; she might have become a successful writer—but now all that potential, Anne's gift for living, had been wiped out. The Nazis saw only the fact that she was Jewish; inflamed by hatred as senseless as it was dangerous, they decided that this was reason enough to kill her.

Mr. Frank came to visit Jacqueline and her parents frequently in the weeks and months following the news of his children's death.

"He cried and cried, and I was at a loss as to how to console him," she remembers. "The only thing I could do was talk to him about his children, and that was really the only thing he wanted. Mr. Frank visited Jetteke often too. Jetteke had been Margot's best friend since before they were both transferred to the Jewish Lyceum, where they were part of a close-knit group, together with another girl named Trees and her boyfriend, Bram. These last three survived the war. Mr. Frank wanted to talk to Jetteke about Margot. He had loved both of his daughters so much."

To know that his children had made such good friends during their short lifetime helped Mr. Frank in his grief. Margot and Anne's friends still missed them and would always remember them.

Mr. Frank also went to visit Anne's friend Lies in the hospital. Mr. Frank had told Jacqueline that Lies and her little sister Gabi had survived and that Lies had been transferred to a hospital in Amsterdam's old Jewish Quarter. Jacqueline went to see her too, not knowing quite what to expect. Lies was on the sixth floor, and when Jacqueline arrived in the room, she saw her lying in bed, a small, quiet figure. It was a strange moment, to meet again after all that had happened. Lies told Jacqueline how she and her family had been sent to Bergen-Belsen, where her father and grandparents had died from the terrible conditions. And she told her that Anne was in Bergen-Belsen too and she was able to talk to her through a fence on two occasions. She didn't hear from her again; now she knew why. Jacqueline listened as Lies explained that she and Gabi had been on a train bound for another concentration camp when they were liberated by the Russians. Lies was sent to a hospital in Maastricht, but Mr. Frank had arranged for her to be brought to Amsterdam. Gabi was being cared for by a family friend.

"When I'm better," Lies said, "Mr. Frank is going to help me get the papers I need to move to Switzerland with Gabi. We have an uncle there. And then, I think we're going to go to Palestine. I can't live here. There are too many memories."

Jacqueline understood what she meant. Although she tried not to think about the past, she was confronted by it at every turn. Her father's grief at losing so many members of his family made him turn to his religion. He spent hour after hour in the synagogue. Neither Jacqueline nor her sister wanted to become Jews again; they simply wanted to try and rebuild their lives. But Jacqueline was very interested in the story of one of the Jewish boys who had returned to the neighborhood after being in hiding in the east of the Netherlands. She recognized him as the other boy with the star who used to play in her street. His name was Ruud, and he was to become Jacqueline's husband.

Jacqueline felt very strongly that she had to move on with her life, and though she mourned the friends she had lost, she was eager to begin living again: "When the war ended I was sixteen years old. I wanted to start afresh and forget those dark years as much as I could."

However, it wasn't going to be as easy as Jacqueline hoped, for on one of his visits, Mr. Frank explained that Miep had saved Anne's diary, and he intended to publish it.

Amsterdam 23 Maart 1942.

Lieve Jacque,

Blijf steeds een zonnestraaltje,

Op school een aardig Kind.

Voor mij mijn liefste vriendinnetje,

Dan wordt je door ieder bemind

Ter herinnering
aan je vriendinnetje

Anne Frank.

A poem written by Anne Frank in Jacqueline's autograph book.

CHAPTER 9

THE DIARY
OF ANNE FRANK

When Mr. Frank first told Jacqueline that Miep had saved Anne's diary, hoping to give it to her when she returned, Jacqueline was surprised, but she didn't want to know any more about it. At one time she had been curious to know what Anne was writing about their friends, but now she felt that she couldn't read it without Anne's permission. How would Anne feel if she knew they were looking at her private thoughts? It didn't seem right somehow, not then. Jacqueline remembered how Anne had never wanted people to look at her diary. Would she feel differently now? However, she could well imagine that having the diary—which Anne had kept throughout the time she was in hiding—was a comfort to Mr. Frank.

He brought the diary along to show Jacqueline. Anne had written so much that the first little book had been quickly filled. She had then used office ledgers, exercise books, and sheets of loose paper. Mr. Frank's face was red with excitement as he told Jacqueline, "Her writing is incredible. I had no idea she had such a gift for words, or that she had developed into such a deep-thinking young woman. I loved her with all my heart and we were very close, but it's only through reading the diary that I feel I've really gotten to know Anne."

Although she felt uncomfortable doing it, Jacqueline glanced at the books to please Mr. Frank. She was intrigued by the great improvement in Anne's handwriting over the years. In the diary, it was clear to see this development. The early pages were covered in a childish, flat scrawl, but the writing gradually changed until the later pages were filled with an elegant, flowing script. Anne had always had a very distinctive way of holding her pen: she held it between her index finger and her middle finger because she had once sprained her thumb. Jacqueline used to copy her and found that her own handwriting improved as a result too. She still wrote the same way, to remind herself of Anne. Seeing how neat and tidy her friend's writing had become made her think about how Anne must have grown up in the years they had been apart. So much time had been lost. . . .

Mr. Frank told Jacqueline that, during their time in hiding, Anne had dreamed about having her diary published. She had begun to rewrite it, giving everyone different names. "She called you 'Jopie,'" Mr. Frank told Jacqueline. Now he intended to honor Anne's wish.

Jacqueline sympathized with him but felt certain no one would want to publish the diary: "I thought, how crazy; who would want to read a book written by such a young child? Also, I couldn't believe that anyone would want to read about the war we had gone through."

Mr. Frank was not to be deterred, and he started to combine Anne's original diary with her second version (which she hadn't completed), to show it to a publisher. While working on it, he called to see Jacqueline. Smiling gently, he handed her two pieces of paper and said, "Anne would have wanted you to have these."

Jacqueline looked down at what he had given her. With a shock, she realized that, at last, she was holding Anne's farewell letter. She waited until she was alone before reading it slowly, taking in every word.

This is the promised farewell letter.

September 25, 1942.

Dear Jacqueline,

I am writing this letter in order to bid you good-bye. That will probably surprise you, but fate has decreed that I must leave (as you will of course have heard a long time ago) with my family, for reasons you will know.

When you telephoned me on Sunday afternoon I couldn't say anything, for my mother had told me not to, the whole house was upside down, and the front door was locked. Hello was due to come, but we didn't answer the door. I can't write to everyone and that's why I'm just writing to you. I'm taking it that you won't talk to anybody about the letter nor from whom you got it. I would be so grateful if you would be really nice and keep up a secret correspondence with me. All enquiries to Mrs. Gies!!!! I hope we'll meet again soon, but it probably won't be before the end of the war. If Lies or anyone else asks you if you've heard anything from me say absolutely nothing, otherwise you'll get us and Mrs. Gies into mortal trouble, so I hope you'll be really careful. Later, of course, you'll be able to tell people that you had a farewell letter from

me. Well then, Jackie, I hope things go well with you,
that I hear from you soon and that we'll meet again
soon.

> *Your <u>best</u> friend,*
> *<u>Anne</u>*

P.S. I hope that we'll always stay <u>best</u> friends until
we meet again.

Trembling with emotion, Jacqueline placed the
sheet of paper down on her lap. Anne must have written it either shortly before entering the hiding place
or perhaps even during that dark, rainy Monday
morning when she spent her last hours in her home
on Merwedeplein, since she had written, "I must
leave." She had probably written a proper letter and
then rewritten it in her diary in September 1942, as
the date showed. Had she left the original somewhere
in her house after all? Jacqueline wondered. But it
didn't matter now—the letter would have vanished
long ago.

Jacqueline picked up the second page and stared at
it in puzzlement. Anne had pretended that she had received an answer from Jacqueline and was writing to
her again:

Second letter

September 25, 1942.

Dear Jackie,

I was very glad to get your letter. If no Germans have been to our apartment so far, please could you go round to Mr. Goldsmith and pick up some of our books and papers and games. You can have them or look after them for me, or else you could take them to Mrs. Gies. I forgot to tell you in my last letter that you must not keep these letters from me because <u>no one</u> must find them. So cut them up into tiny pieces, just like we did that time with the letter from Mummy's box. Please do it. How are you all? I mustn't write about myself of course. I think of you so often. How is Ilse, is she still around? I've heard from Mrs. Gies that Lies is still here. We're not bored and we have company, I mustn't write anything more about our life until later, although it is weird but interesting. This letter mustn't get too long. Be seeing you and a little kiss from
<u>*Anne*</u>

The letter from Mummy's box. Jacqueline smiled sadly, remembering all the times she and Anne had sat on the gravel roof terrace at Merwedeplein, sunning themselves and telling each other secrets, giggling away. If they had known then what the future held. . . .

Today Jacqueline thinks that Anne wrote those letters, including the second one, because she must have found the thought of being in hiding until the war ended, without her friends, unbearable: "She must have been so lonely, inventing my answer to her when I had never been able to contact her after she left Merwedeplein. But I'm so glad that she wrote those letters and copied them into her diary. They show how much our friendship still meant to her. From the letters it's clear that her disappointment in my behavior, over her jealousy, was just a passing thing and everything was okay again. That was a comfort to me."

At first Mr. Frank struggled to find a publisher for the diary, just as Jacqueline had imagined he might. "They all say that interest in the war is as dead as a doornail," he explained to Jacqueline. "It isn't that Anne's writing isn't good enough to be published, it's simply that people don't want to read anything connected to the war, and especially what happened to Jewish people. Everybody wants to move on, to forget."

Jacqueline found this understandable, for these were her own feelings too. But then an article about the diary by a well-known historian was published in a Dutch newspaper, and this sparked interest in the book.

Mr. Frank called Jacqueline and invited her to lunch: "I've got something important to tell you, and something to ask you too," he said.

They met in a café in the city center. Mr. Frank looked nervous, but excited too. When they were having lunch, he told Jacqueline, "I've got a publisher for the diary! They're going to bring it out in a year's time. I have to pay part of the costs, but that doesn't matter. And Jacqueline"—he paused and took her hand before going on in his soft voice—"they'd like you to write something about your friendship with Anne for it."

Jacqueline didn't know what to say, but her mind raced. What could she write? Would anyone want to read about their passion for reading, playing Monopoly together for hours on end, or the fact that they both collected pictures of movie stars? What about Anne's curiosity regarding relationships between men and women, or her belief that every boy she met fell in love with her? They were private memories too.

Jacqueline gave Mr. Frank's hand a squeeze and said gently but firmly, "I'm so sorry, Mr. Frank, but I can't do it. I don't think anyone will be interested and . . . I just can't. Please forgive me."

Mr. Frank shook his head. "It's fine, don't worry, Jacqueline. The publisher came up with the idea, not me. If you don't want to do it, that's up to you."

Relieved, Jacqueline changed the subject.

In 1947 the diary was published under the title Anne had wanted for it, *Het Achterhuis* ("The House Behind" in Dutch). Mr. Frank gave Jacqueline a copy with a personal note, which she stuck inside the front flap so that she wouldn't lose it.

At first, Jacqueline couldn't read the book. It was a summer's afternoon, and the sun shone brightly on the windows, making a pool of yellow light on the floor next to the chair where Jacqueline sat like a tightly curled spring. I can't do this! she thought wildly. I can't read Anne's diary without her permission. But then she remembered that Mr. Frank had said that Anne's greatest wish was to be a writer. She had wanted people to read her words; she had wanted to go on living after her death.

Jacqueline took a deep breath, relaxed her shoulders, and opened the book. "On Friday June 12, I woke up at six o'clock and no wonder; it was my birthday. . . ." Jacqueline felt the years fall away and let herself go back in time to 1942 and Anne's birthday party. There it all was, in Anne's own words, and there she was too, under the name Jopie: "For years Lies Goosens and Sanne Houtmann have been my best friends. Since then, I've got to know Jopie de Waal at the Jewish Secondary School and she is now my best girl friend. . . . "

Jacqueline read about the Little Bear Minus 2 Club: "We ping-pongers are very partial to an ice cream, especially in summer when one gets warm at the game, so we usually finish up with a visit to the nearest ice-cream shop, 'Delphi' or 'Oasis,' where Jews are allowed. . . . " Jacqueline saw them all: herself, Anne, Sanne, Ilse, and Lies walking across Merwede-plein and over to Oasis, the sun on their backs as they laughed and joked about which boys might be hanging around there.

She went back to the diary: "After May 1940, good times rapidly fled: first the war, then the capitulation, followed by the arrival of the Germans. That's when the suffering of us Jews really began . . . Jopie used to say to me: 'You're scared to do anything, because it may be forbidden. . . . '" Jacqueline had a vivid picture of herself and Anne sitting on the steps of their school, yellow stars glaring from their clothes.

She returned to the book and found herself reading about the moment when the call-up came for Margot, and then how the whole family had gone into hiding in the annex behind Mr. Frank's workplace, by the side of the Prinsengracht Canal. She read on and on, amazed by the fluidity of Anne's words, her gift for capturing every aspect of their lives in hiding. She read about Anne's falling in love with Peter van Pels, her faith in God, the way she had changed from a girl into a young woman, her hope that they would be freed so that she could go back to school and finish her education, and her fear that they would be discovered by the Gestapo in the end.

She came to the next-to-last entry: "Now I am really getting hopeful, now things are going well at last." Jacqueline felt numb; just as Anne had allowed herself to believe that freedom was near, they had been betrayed. She read the last few lines, in which Anne described how she wanted to be something better than she showed herself to be, but how difficult that was when everyone had already judged her: "I twist my heart around again, so that the bad is on the outside and the good is on the inside, and keep on trying to find a way of becoming what I would so like to be, and what I could be, if . . . there weren't any other people living in the world."

Jacqueline closed the book. The summer evening was drawing to an end and it was almost dark outside, apart from the dramatic orange glow that was all that was left of the sunset on the horizon. She switched on the lamp and looked down at the book again. Although she felt great sadness over losing Anne, she was glad that Mr. Frank had published her diary. "Anne's passion and zest for life, so familiar to me back then, echoed through to the very last pages of the book. Even her belief in the goodness of people and in a better world hadn't disappeared during the years she spent in hiding. I shared her belief then." Jacqueline was pleased that her real name was not used in the book: "No one knew I had been Anne's best friend and, as far as I was concerned, it could stay that way." Her friendship with Anne was something she didn't want to discuss; it was all too painful, and her shyness would have made it impossible.

In 1952 Jacqueline moved to England, working for six months as a nanny for a couple in London who had a three-year-old daughter. The mother wrote children's books and the father was a magazine editor. One day he arrived home clutching a book, which he handed to Jacqueline, saying, "This was written by a Dutch girl; you might find it interesting." Jacqueline's eyes widened: it was Anne's diary.

Later that evening, she read the book for the second time, in its English translation. To her surprise, she saw that there were passages in the book that hadn't been in the Dutch edition. In one paragraph Anne had written about how curious she had been over Jacqueline's body when they were growing up, and how she had given Jacqueline a quick kiss. Thank goodness it wasn't in the Dutch edition! Jacqueline thought. It would have been a bit embarrassing if someone who knew me read that.

At breakfast the following morning, her employers asked her if she had found the book interesting. "Yes," said Jacqueline, hesitantly. "Yes, I did." She wondered if she should tell them that she had known Anne and was actually in the book herself.

A few days later, a friend of the British couple came to stay, and Jacqueline asked her if she would like to read the diary. The woman pulled her mouth into a disapproving line and said curtly, "No." That made Jacqueline think twice about mentioning the diary to anyone. She couldn't face that sort of prejudice again, and decided to stay silent about her past.

After living with Miep and Jan Gies for several years, Mr. Frank moved to Basel in Switzerland to be with his remaining family, but he always kept in touch with Jacqueline. Whenever he was in the Netherlands, he would call her and they would sometimes meet up. Mr. Frank was usually accompanied by his second wife, Fritzi, who had survived Auschwitz with her daughter but had lost her first husband and son in the camps. Mr. Frank continued to be very affectionate toward Jacqueline, and often brought her small gifts. When he offered to show Jacqueline around their former hiding place on Prinsengracht, she accepted.

It was an emotional experience for Jacqueline to walk through the old offices with Mr. Frank, and then along a corridor where a bookcase stood slightly away from the wall, revealing a small gray door. Mr. Frank explained how the bookcase had been made by one of their helpers. It was designed to hide the entrance to the annex, and could be opened by those who knew where to find the secret latch.

Jacqueline stepped up into the annex; it was very stuffy and quite dark, despite the clear skies. Mr. Frank guided her into the room he had shared with his wife and Margot, and pointed out the marks on the wall where he had measured Anne's growth during the hiding period. There was a map beside the pencil lines.

"I put this here," Mr. Frank explained. "It shows the Allied advance. They were so close to us, that summer. But it was not to be."

Jacqueline said nothing, following him into the next room, which was narrower than the one before.

"This was Anne's room," Mr. Frank said softly. "You

might recognize one or two of the pictures."

Jacqueline nodded, amazed. She had read in the diary how Anne had stuck postcards and pictures to the walls of her room in the annex, to make it "more cheerful," but it was still something of a shock, and very moving, to see them. "That was something that belonged to the two of us," Jacqueline recalls. "We built up our collections together." She walked up to the walls to see if there were many postcards she recognized. There were two photographs of the British queen and her sister as young children that Jacqueline had given to Anne in exchange for a Shirley Temple postcard, and many photographs of movie stars and some pictures of beautiful dresses. Jacqueline was speechless.

Looking at the pictures on the fading wallpaper of Anne's room in the secret annex was like looking at ghosts.

Jacqueline with Otto Frank in his garden
in Basel, Switzerland, in 1970.

CHAPTER 10

FAME

Anne's diary became a worldwide best-seller, translated into scores of languages. A play based on it opened in America, and in November 1956 it had its premiere in Amsterdam. Mr. Frank invited Jacqueline and Margot's best friend, Jetteke, to the opening night. "Jopie" was mentioned during the play. It was a very strange moment for Jacqueline, who turned to look at Ruud, whom she had married after returning from England. After the play, a Hollywood film was made, and the house where Anne had hidden was opened as a museum.

Jacqueline tried to keep out of the limelight as much as possible. Naturally shy and reserved, she found it odd that people wanted to know about her friendship with Anne. Jacqueline recalls, "When my daughter was twelve, she asked me whether she could finally tell her friends that her mother was the Jopie of the diary. Sometimes my husband would raise the topic as well, and a look from me wasn't always enough to silence him."

As the years passed, and the diary became more and more famous, Jacqueline saw how Anne had become a symbol of all those murdered in the Holocaust. It was very odd indeed to think that the girl with whom she had shared secrets and played Monopoly was known by millions of people.

Mr. Frank made sure that he sent Jacqueline copies of everything published about Anne. When new editions of her diary and the stories she had written in hiding were published, he sent her those too. Jacqueline sometimes visited Mr. Frank at his lovely home in Basel. There he showed her his office, where he and Fritzi answered all the letters sent to them by readers of the diary. The two of them traveled all over the world to talk about Anne and to educate people against racism and prejudice. Jacqueline frequently received postcards from them telling her about their work and the people they met.

On one of his visits to the Netherlands, Mr. Frank told Jacqueline that there was quite a lot of the diary that hadn't been published. He allowed her to see these missing entries, which Jacqueline read with interest, sorrow, and, sometimes, amusement. She read what Anne had written about their former classmates at the Jewish Lyceum, which wasn't always flattering, and discovered that Anne had known about her visit to the house on Merwedeplein with Lies. She was also very surprised to find that a New Year's card she had sent Anne was pasted onto a page of the diary. Alongside it Anne had written, "This is the only letter I had from Jacqueline van Maarsen, I asked her often enough for a photograph and she said she would look one out for me, but now on September 28, 1942 it is too late. . . . This is the only written token of Jacqueline's friendship, apart from my poor autograph album. She is being very nice again at the moment and I hope things will stay like that. I now think quite differently about the things I wrote down earlier . . . all I want to do is to apologize and to explain things." Those words made Jacqueline feel much happier, for she could see that Anne had forgotten their silly arguments, and it made the memory of their close friendship even more precious.

In July 1980, Jacqueline and Ruud visited Mr. Frank in Basel and found him lying in bed, desperately ill with cancer. Jacqueline knew then that she would never see him again and found it hard to say good-bye. A month later Jacqueline heard an announcement on the radio that Mr. Frank was dead. Although it did not come as a shock, Jacqueline was still very upset. Her husband was away, so she sat quietly alone, thinking back to all the times she had spent with Mr. Frank, remembering his courage and kindness over the years.

After Mr. Frank's death, the foundations he had established in Amsterdam (the Anne Frank Stichting, responsible for the upkeep of the house where the Franks had hidden) and Switzerland (the Anne Frank-Fonds, which donates the income from sales of the diary to various charitable causes) continued the work he had begun. The Anne Frank House became more and more popular with tourists and is now the Netherlands' second most visited museum. In 1985 an exhibition about Anne's life, the Holocaust, and the diary opened in Amsterdam, and Jacqueline was presented to the Dutch queen as Anne's best friend. Afterwards she smiled to herself: "I thought how splendid Anne would have thought it was that because of *her* book I received an introduction to the queen!"

In 1986 Anne's complete diaries were published, partly to dispel accusations that they were fakes; scientific tests proved beyond doubt that they were genuine. Jacqueline allowed her real name to be published in the interests of historical accuracy, and since then she has become a more public figure. She has written two books and occasionally gives interviews about Anne and speeches about her experiences during the war. Her husband, Ruud, accompanies her everywhere and gives talks about his life in hiding. Jacqueline has been involved in several films about Anne, and for one documentary she had to revisit all the familiar places of her childhood. She even went inside Anne's apartment on Merwedeplein again, which gave her a strange feeling. The apartment had been slightly modernized, but then she saw the gravel terrace where she and Anne had giggled and gossiped during the first summer days of 1942. Jacqueline also visited the Jewish Lyceum and found herself becoming very emotional as she walked around the old playground, shading her eyes from the glint of the sun on the Amstel River: "Memories that I had always suppressed resurfaced: of a playground full of children that grew steadily empty over the course of a year. . . ."

At home again, when filming for the documentary was over, Jacqueline remembered something Anne had written in a short story about wanting to be a movie star: "One way or another everyone will know my name later." The thought sent a shiver through Jacqueline, and she turned to Anne's diary for comfort. She found it there in a few short lines that took her back to those happy days when they had first met at school and their wonderful friendship had begun:

> Well then, Jackie, I hope things go well with you, that I hear from you soon and that we'll meet again soon.
>
> Your <u>best</u> friend,
> <u>Anne</u>
>
> P.S. I hope that we'll always stay <u>best</u> friends until we meet again.

"We will, Anne, I promise," Jacqueline said softly, and closed the book.

TIMELINE OF
IMPORTANT EVENTS
IN THE NETHERLANDS

In 1933 Adolf Hitler and his National Socialist Party came to power in Germany. The party's members, and people who supported its views, were called Nazis. Hitler blamed Germany's hard times on the Jews, and in 1935 his government passed the Nuremberg Laws, which made life very difficult for the Jews of Germany. On November 9 and 10, 1938, in retaliation for the murder of a German diplomat, the Nazis launched an attack on Jewish homes, businesses, and synagogues throughout Germany, Austria, and the Sudentenland (part of the Czech Republic). The attack became known as Kristallnacht—the Night of Broken Glass. Then, in 1939, Germany invaded Poland, and as a result, France and Britain declared war on Germany. The Second World War had begun.

1 9 4 0

MAY 10: Germany invades the Netherlands.

MAY 15: The Dutch surrender.

OCT 22: Jewish businesses forced to register with the Nazi authorities.

NOV 21: Jews are fired from all government and civil service positions.

1 9 4 1

JAN 10: Everyone "wholly or largely of Jewish blood" forced to register with the Nazi authorities.

FEB 22: First group of Jews in Amsterdam are rounded up and imprisoned.

FEB 25–26: Workers in Amsterdam go on strike to protest the mistreatment of Jews. The strike is ended by declaration of martial law.

MAY 1: Jewish doctors, pharmacists, and translators banned from working for non-Jews. Jews no longer allowed to own radios. Jews banned

from attending stock and commercial
exchanges.

MAY 31: Jews banned from using swimming pools
and public parks.

JUNE 11: More Jews in Amsterdam rounded up.

JUNE–AUG: Jews required to place their bank accounts and
property in a Nazi-controlled bank, and many
are forced to sell their businesses to non-Jews.

SEPT 1: Jewish children forced to attend separate
schools.

SEPT 15: Jews no longer allowed to visit zoos, cafés,
restaurants, hotels, guest houses, theaters,
cinemas, concerts, or libraries.

NOV 7: Jews banned from traveling or moving to
a new residence without permission.

1942

JAN 1: Jews no longer allowed to employ non-
Jewish domestic servants.

JAN 10: First Jews from Amsterdam sent to work
camps.

MAR 25 : Marriage between Jews and non-Jews banned.

APRIL 24 : Most Jewish butchers' shops closed down.

MAY 2 : Jewish star on clothes introduced.

JUNE 12 : Jews made to hand in bicycles and other transport. All forms of sports forbidden for Jews.

JUNE 30 : Jews must stay indoors after 8:00 P.M. Jews banned from using public transportation or telephones.

JULY 5 : First call-up notices sent out for "labor services in Germany," including one to Margot Frank. This is the beginning of the mass deportations to the death camps.

JULY 14 : Seven hundred Jews in Amsterdam randomly arrested.

JULY 15 : First trainload of Jews leaves Amsterdam for deportation to Auschwitz concentration camp in Poland.

AUG 9 : Further raids carried out on Jews in Amsterdam.

SEPT 15: Jewish students banned from almost all institutions of higher education.

1943

MAY 26: Mass roundup carried out in Amsterdam to capture remaining Jews. Deportations continue throughout the year.

DEC 29: The Netherlands declared largely "Jew-free."

1944

SEPT 6: Last group of Dutch Jews, including Anne Frank and her family, are sent to concentration camps.

1945

MAY 5: Entire Netherlands officially liberated.